Recalling Religions

Recalling Religions

*Resistance, Memory, and
Cultural Revision in
Ethnic Women's
Literature*

PETER KERRY POWERS

THE UNIVERSITY OF
TENNESSEE PRESS

KNOXVILLE

Excerpts from *The Woman Warrior* by Maxine Hong Kingston. Copyright © 1975, 1976 by Maxine Hong Kingston. Reprinted by permission of Alfred A. Knopf, a Division of Random House Inc. British Commonwealth rights granted by the author and the Sandra Dijkstra Literary Agency.
Excerpts from *Levitation: Five Fictions* by Cynthia Ozick. Copyright © 1982 by Cynthia Ozick. Reprinted by permission of Alfred A. Knopf, a Division of Random House Inc. British Commonwealth rights granted by Raines and Raines.
Excerpts from *The Shawl* by Cynthia Ozick. Copyright © 1980, 1981 by Cynthia Ozick. Reprinted by permission of Alfred A. Knopf, a Division of Random House Inc. British Commonwealth rights granted by Raines and Raines.
Excerpts from *Ceremony* by Leslie Marmon Silko. Copyright © 1977 by Leslie Marmon Silko. Reprinted by permission of Viking Penguin, a division of Penguin Putnam Inc.
"In These Dissenting Times," copyright © 1971 by Alice Walker, reprinted by permission of Harcourt, Inc. British Commonwealth rights granted by David Higham Associates.
Permission to reprint portions of chapter two granted by *MELUS: The Journal of the Society for the Study of Multi-ethnic Literatures of the United States.*
Permission to reprint portions of chapter three granted by *South Atlantic Review.*

The paper used in this book meets the minimum requirements of ANSI/NISO Z39.48-1992 (R 1997) (Permanence of Paper). The binding materials have been chosen for strength and durability.

Library of Congress Cataloging-in-Publication Data

Powers, Peter Kerry, 1959–
Recalling religions : resistance, memory, and cultural revision in
ethnic women's literature / Peter Kerry Powers.— 1st ed.
    p. cm.
Includes bibliographical references (p.   ) and index.
ISBN 1-57233-127-5 (hardcover : alk. paper)

1. American fiction—Minority authors—History and criticism. 2. Religion and literature—United States—History—20th century. 3. Women and literature—United States—History—20th century. 4. American fiction—Women authors—History and criticism. 5. American fiction—20th century—History and criticism. 6. Religious fiction, American—History and criticism. 7. Walker, Alice, 1944-   —Religion. 8. Silko, Leslie, 1948-   —Religion. 9. Kingston, Maxine Hong—Religion. 10. Ethnic groups in literature. 11. Ozick, Cynthia—Religion. 12. Religion in literature. 13. Memory in literature. I. Title.

PS374.R47 P69 2001
813'.54099287'08693—dc21   00-012032

IN MEMORY OF JOSEPH MCCLATCHEY, MY BEST TEACHER

CONTENTS

Acknowledgments

It would be impossible to mention all the people that have contributed to the changing journey that writing this book has become. Certainly I must mention my best teacher, Joe McClatchey, who in introducing me to the monomyth also introduced me to the whole world of literature and its differences. Jane Tompkins's insistence on excellence and her willingness to take seriously my interests in religion and literature helped me survive the intellectual maelstrom that was Duke University in the 1980s and 1990s. Tom Ferraro and Kenneth Surin have both been sources of intellectual and personal inspiration. I also thank Joseph Skerrett and Julia Kasdorf for their consistent encouragement. Their readings contributed to what clarity and consistency I have been able to muster. Joyce Harrison at the University of Tennessee Press has kept me moving with her encouragement. The close readings by the readers at the Press helped me see clearly the book that lay in the draft I had sent to them. I thank those journals that have furthered my work along the way: an earlier form of the chapter on Ozick appeared in *MELUS* and an earlier form of the chapter on Alice Walker appeared in *South Atlantic Review*. My institution, Messiah College, has provided funds to keep me working in the summers. I thank my parents for never giving up on me. Finally, I thank Shannon, my wife, and my two children, Devon Elizabeth and Colin Daniel, who have put up with more than a few Saturdays alone and who help me remember there are a few things more important than reading and writing.

INTRODUCTION

Learning from Leon Uris:
Literature, Difference, and Change

In simplest terms, this book is about religion, memory, and cultural resistance in literature written by ethnic women. However, in my imagination, the story of this book's motivations, interests, and point of view threads back to my first encounters with literature, which always seemed to be troublesome encounters with religion as well. My earliest memories of something that might be called "literature" had nothing to do with Twain or Fenimore Cooper or other authors of "boys' books" that serious young readers were supposed to read. Indeed, I barely knew of their existence. What I did know was tangled with agonized parental debates—probably exaggerated in my memory—as to what was appropriate for a young boy from a holiness church to read. As late as eighth grade, I remember standing alone and wistful at my homeroom window watching my classmates board a bus for the local theater to see Robert Redford in *The Great Gatsby*. The chances of attending the film had been slim in the first place, since our church forbade movies along with dancing and drinking as contrary to holy living. Still, I had my hopes. School, combined with the responsibility my parents felt to help their smart children be successful in the world, had always been a slick oil with which I could slip through the narrowest confines of home. *The Great Gatsby* was a classic novel, or so I assured my parents that the teacher had assured me. Such appeals to the greatness of Western culture lost what little cachet they possessed when my mother discovered that in Fitzgerald's novel a woman's breast is torn off by a car.

My mother wanted her son seeing neither breasts nor violence. And so, when I pull my copy of *The Great Gatsby* off the shelf—a book I did not read until my years as an English major at a Christian college—it is this rather self-pitying memory of me at a window that I see most clearly. For the most part, the dead white male writers and their cinematic representations remained far too worldly for a young holiness boy threatened on every side by the corruption of suburban Oklahoma City.

Nevertheless, if I did not come to the Western canon early, I did read what I could get my hands on, absorbed by the world of difference that reading seemed to offer. The son of missionaries, I spent my earliest years in what is now Papua New Guinea, addicted not to television, which was nowhere to be found, but to the *World Book Encyclopedia*, which I read from A to Z.

Returning to the United States during third grade, I devoured the novels of missionary lives and of the lives of church heroes and heroines, books made available weekly on Wednesday nights after prayer meeting. Clair Bee's novels about sports heroes and Hardy Boys mysteries, the authentic originals with hardback blue covers, were part of the mix, perhaps deemed innocuous entertainment better than television. The closest I came to classic fiction was in Edgar Rice Burroughs's Tarzan novels after my grandfather rescued a collection of well-thumbed first editions from his attic.

A few months after missing out on Robert Redford, I lost myself in the novels of Leon Uris, a serious concession my parents deemed appropriate because they told of the plight of the Jews. On a long summer vacation in the car, I sat reading Uris's treatise on the Warsaw ghetto, *Mila 18*, listening to my parents as they whispered and worried; perhaps they sensed that in the pages of that novel I escaped them somehow, and they worried that their concession to the demands of their thirteen-year-old's imaginative appetite was a step too far. I remember, quite vividly, the breathless scene in which the hero and heroine disregard their moral heritage, strip one another's clothes, and make love in a desperate fever. Looking back as a literary and cultural critic, it is hard to recapture that fever through the screen of Uris's turgid prose. But at the time, my erotically driven imagination felt that sex was somehow political and that the received morality might not apply in every circumstance. Somehow, this novel—usually deemed so much pop and fizz by whomever decides such things—reconfirmed what I always already knew: reading, almost any reading, could be a transgression.

I tell this story of a reading life to suggest the twin and sometimes conflicting urgencies that drove the writing of this book, urgencies that are, it seems to me, useful windows into the particular problems of thinking about religion and ethnic literature. On the one hand, reading has always seemed to me to be about the encounter with difference. Thus, however much I have employed the insights of the hermeneutics of suspicion in this book, I think an interpretive methodology that does not account for literature's transgressiveness has missed something crucial about the act of reading. Reading literature does not merely confirm one's own horizons, however much those horizons must be the only possible point of departure. Reading challenges and changes horizons as well. Thus, while my readings in this book were formed because of my personal religious interests, commitments, and history, this literature has also intrigued and changed me because of the inescapable difference from my own experience. In reading Maxine Hong Kingston or Leslie Silko, I encountered imaginative worlds similar to and different from my own and have been forced, in however limited a way, to reassess my own imaginative world. Particularly, reading this literature over time has partially delivered me from the existential Christian individualism that dominated my imaginative life during my college years and their immediate aftermath—a time when I loved Kierkegaard, Updike, O'Connor, Percy, to name only a few. Seen in this way, the difference that literature always insists on is not a liability to understanding, but a great gift, one of the most important reasons for reading in the first place.

On the other hand, the act of reading, of encountering and accounting for difference, is more complicated than this simple assertion of appreciation suggests. As my brief biography indicates, reading does not take place in a vacuum, but within a variety of constraining contexts. Among the most obvious constraints is what one is allowed to read or forbidden to read. For the past twenty-five years Stanley Fish has argued that the constraints of a community are enabling constraints without which we would be unable to read at all. Following in this line Robert Detweiler has imagined reading as a communal activity in which "a reader understands herself as part of a community engaged in simultaneously recognizing, criticizing, and reshaping the myths and rituals it lives by" (*Breaking* 38). I am sympathetic to both of these views, and, indeed, my book proposes that many ethnic women have used religion to critically engage the individualism so central to the traditional canons of American liter- ature and to traditions of reading that canon. Nonetheless, not all constraints enable equally. For a very long time in American history women and slaves were forbidden or otherwise discouraged from reading at all: a constraint to be sure. But using Fish and Detweiler I could not critically engage or judge between this and other con- straints, such as that which discouraged men from reading novels in the nineteenth century. Detweiler's generous vision seems to elide the fact that communities read within the context of exclusionary hier- archies of power and use the processes of reading to reinforce those hierarchies of power. While reading as a child, I came to understand what was desirable not simply by what my community allowed me to read but also by what it forbade me to read. Thus, missionary novels and F. Scott Fitzgerald had similar functions in some respects, but the horizon of desire which they invoked cut across the readerly expectations of my community in very different ways. One taught me how I ought to behave; the other represented that dark area beyond the limit of the community's self-understanding.

Realistically, the question of reading lesbians, gays, ethnic others, Buddhists, or anything else that provokes contemporary debate about the canon was moot for my religious community. For a very long time, Ernest Hemingway was the problem, not Alice Walker.

Nevertheless, difference does make its way, in part because we belong to many communities. If I did not get to see Robert Redford in his youthful glory, I did attend other movies at a summer camp, a place where I and my parents learned that some Christians did go to movies and even dance. Walter Cronkite brought Vietnam and burn- ing Buddhist priests into my living room just like any other American living room. We are no longer a village. Difference is everywhere and must be read and understood.

This fact of unavoidable difference presents a slightly different problem for a community of readers. One fairly common response is to read difference as just so much more of the same. For instance,

Leon Uris can be read and appreciated by conservative Christians because his Jewish nationalist vision and his celebration of Jewish resistance during the Holocaust comport well with conservative evangelical visions of the end times. Among conservative Christians, this is a time when Israel will face the persecution of the nations and be restored to the Holy Land, all of which foreshadows the second coming of Christ. Thus Uris's "Jewishness" is relatively inconsequential to such readers because these events in Jewish history foretell the coming reign of Christ, a period in which every particular Jewish person will be revealed as, in fact, a proto-Christian. Read in this way, Uris is not so much about Jewish nationalism as about Christian prophecy. This confirms the communitarian reading theories of Fish and Detweiler, but it also makes it difficult to distinguish between acts of creative appropriation and imaginative imperialism. One often reads in the default drive of the community to easily avoid the challenges that difference can offer.

It has seemed to me that academic readings of religion in ethnic women's literature have suffered from an oddly similar tendency toward homogenization. In my academic life, this method of reducing otherness to sameness received a more rigorous theoretical grounding during my years at Wheaton College, a self-described bastion of Christian evangelicalism. While I was there, Northrop Frye's myth criticism reigned, serving both to open the Christian reader to "non-Christian" literature and to neuter the difference such literature might have invoked. Believing in a version of the monomyth, we could read almost anything, but we were not ultimately threatened by much of anything since the monomyth always ultimately pointed to Christ.

While the specifics of this version of interpretation were probably unique to evangelical Christian circles, I kept feeling an eerie sense of déjà vu as I read through the criticism of religion and ethnic women's literature in preparation for this book. What had seemed most interesting to me in the first place—the uniqueness and singularity of the visions I was encountering—kept being re-created as something else: sometimes the Christian monomyth, sometimes the "universally human," most often a vaguely defined "Religion" that usually seemed to be a version of the other two. Often unrecognized, a quasi-structuralist version of Religion has driven investigations of this literature, and the particularity of traditions has been squeezed to fit the structure. Recognizing this, I have worked with a method that recognizes the horizon of similarity that exists between these works of ethnic literature while also insisting on the uniqueness that derives from specific traditions and gives a particular accent to each writer's engagement with the multiple cultures of the United States.

The first chapter, "Beneath the Table: Religion, Ethnicity, and American Literary Studies," lays out this problem of reading religion and literature in greater detail. In sum, I suggest that where religion has not been ignored in the reading of ethnic women's literature it has been terribly reduced, and where religion has been central to a critical enterprise it has often proceeded with a theory of "Religion" that precludes any serious engagement with ethnic religious traditions and histories. Over and against this tendency I have suggested that recognizing the narrative underpinnings of religious traditions and of literary works allows us to maintain the specificity of traditions while also recognizing those points where they overlap with one another and with the still powerful traditions of the canons of American literature. The writers I take up, Leslie Silko, Cynthia Ozick, Maxine Hong Kingston, and Alice Walker, come from very different religious backgrounds, all of which are more or less marginal to the dominant Euro-American Christian traditions within the United States. At the same time, these writers all write in English and appropriate elements from the traditions of Western literature in the forms of short story, novel, and memoir. To various degrees they also embrace underlying ideologies of American liberal democracy that are in tension with particular religious traditions. Thus, their work exists in a space of tension between similarity and difference. This tension leaves them unassimilable to a monomyth that would read them only in terms of Christianity, "Religion," or the universally human.

Because I believe this space of tension must be maintained, I have followed the opening chapter with individual readings of each author. In doing so I have attempted to delineate connections between the authors or between each author and other well-known authors on the American scene. At the same time, I have sought to delineate the specific difference of each author's religious heritage. Through this tension between similarity and difference, each writer critiques American society while at the same time critiquing and rewriting her received religious tradition. The direction of critique obviously varies for each author, given the unique circumstances of biography, ethnic background, and religious commitment. For Cynthia Ozick, both assimilation and the Holocaust threaten the continuity of Jewish cultural memory. The invocation of tradition works against such forgetfulness while also implicitly challenging the traditional Jewish exclusion of women from textual traditions of the people. For Alice Walker the problem is not so much loss of cultural memories as the presence of religious memories that force her female characters to denigrate or dismiss the experience of their own bodies. My reading of Walker's *The Color Purple* suggests that the novel invokes the traditions of Christian justice and transcendence so central to the black church while also using those same traditions to critique Christianity's denigration of women. Like Cynthia Ozick, Leslie Silko recognizes the role of forgetfulness in the destruction of culture as well as the role of religion in maintaining cultural memories. Unlike either Ozick or Walker, however, the problems with remembrance in Silko's work are tied to the specifics of place. Silko invokes religious mythologies to point out the failure to be mindful of the earth in contemporary society but also seeks to envision a Native American community that no longer bears the same relationship to the land as its ancestors. In both *Ceremony* and *Almanac of the Dead* she imagines the possibilities of "changing the ceremonies" to provide for a continuity with tradition that recognizes change and does not live embedded in the past. Finally, Maxine Hong Kingston invokes both traditional Chinese understandings of selfhood as a "self-with-others" and American forms of individualism to envision the possibility of a community that will not deny her the possibility of self-expression as a Chinese American woman.

In the end, Kingston's work, and indeed the work of all these writers, pushes us to recognize the limitations of common Western understandings of Religion and its role in personal, cultural, and political life. Their work does not allow us to collapse difference into an easy familiarity with the same. Neither, however, do these writers allow us to ignore them as if their work were someone else's concern, existing somewhere on the rim of the wheel, the special province of a particular group or someone with a particular ideological bent. Rather, in this tension between similarity and difference, between sameness and otherness, these texts evoke the uncomfortable spaces where the best of literature has always dwelled. These spaces of tension are precisely those places that allow us to encounter the possibility of change. This is, I think, the best that great literature can hope for.

Recalling Religions

1

Beneath the Table

RELIGION, ETHNICITY, AND
AMERICAN LITERARY
STUDIES

A long and rather difficult relationship between religion and the study of culture has created peculiar problems for literary studies, particularly the study of ethnic literature. On the one hand, the modern social sciences have long eschewed "Religion" as an unscientific means of explaining human behavior. On the other hand, Religion seems, annoyingly, to hang around at modernity's party, a ghost unwilling to fade quietly into the long night of the past. One does not get far into the study of culture before religion rattles its chains, whether in popular fascination with angels and appearances of the Virgin Mary or in more abstruse and mind-bending links between deconstruction and mysticism.

More pertinent for my study is the fact that religions of various kinds also continue to provide resources for all manner of political action, and they continue to be linked in interesting ways to the manifestation of ethnic cultural distinction. So strong are these links that Martin Marty has suggested that ethnicity is the backbone of religion in America, and religion is the backbone of ethnicity ("Skeleton" 225). Despite such claims, continuing uneasiness about religion may suggest the limits of academia's celebration of multiculturalism. While

1

differences in forms of dance, music, and language may be embraced, the particularities of religious belief are held uncertainly at arm's length. In Western intellectual history this uneasiness has colored assessments of both ethnicity and religion. Even in relatively "positive" assessments of religion, this ambiguity shines through. Walter Benjamin perceived the potential in religious narratives and attempted to envision a powerful relationship between theology and liberatory political practice. In one familiar reference, Benjamin tells the story of a hunchbacked chess player.

> The story is told of an automaton constructed in such a way that it could play a winning game of chess, answering each move of an opponent with a countermove. A puppet in Turkish attire and with a hookah in its mouth sat before a chessboard placed on a large table. A system of mirrors created the illusion that this table was transparent from all sides. Actually, a little hunchback who was an expert chess player sat inside and guided the puppet's hand by means of strings. One can imagine a philosophical counterpart to this device. The puppet called "historical materialism" is to win all the time. It can easily be a match for anyone if it enlists the services of theology, which today, as we know, is wizened and has to keep out of sight. (253)

Benjamin's image is at once insightful and conflicted. Religion here is all-powerful and wizened but invisible. Indeed, the hunchback's power depends upon his disappearance. Further, the ethnic "Turk" is merely body without mind or spirit, a standard Western configuration of ethnic otherness. However, the Turk is also the presence of an absence, in this case the absence of theology, or discourse about God. On the one hand, ethnicity is the only body by which such discourse can make itself present in the world from which it is otherwise excluded. Thus, in another fairly standard formulation, ethnicity embodies those human things—whether sexuality, community, vernacular languages, or religious traditions—that the West no longer sees in itself. Nevertheless, the ethnic other "lives" only by virtue of "theology," a universalizing discourse represented by the European hunchback.

Though set in Europe, the conundrums presented by Benjamin's famous image are characteristic of the often uneasy relationships between ethnicity, religion, and cultural studies in America. Like the wizened dwarf, religion is often excluded from "appropriate" academic discourse unless disguised in the garb of folk traditions, ethnic cultures, or the language of ideology. But if religion does make its presence felt, the moving body of ethnicity falls limp as attention is given to the apparently more "universal" and disembodied concerns of religion and theology. In the balance of this chapter I want to analyze the consequences of this uneasy relationship for the study of literature written by ethnic women. I further want to suggest some different metaphors to guide cultural analysis, metaphors that might allow us to see the religious traditions of ethnic cultures as an intrinsic part of their particularity.

The Institutions of Literature

Attending to the first element of this dynamic, that of the disappearance of religion, a cursory examination of the average undergraduate anthology of literature "reveals" religion's absence. For instance, *The Harper American Literature* registers the supposed march of American culture away from not only Christianity but also any religious tradition whatsoever. The early portions of the anthology contain some narratives and poetry which would now be considered explicitly religious: Iroquois and Eskimo creation myths, the prose of William Bradford, John Winthrop, and Cotton Mather, a sermon from Jonathan Edwards. So much could only be expected. What is less clear is why religious narratives begin to drop gradually from view until they are nearly absent by the twentieth century. Native American stories drop from the anthology save for single entries from Momaday and Silko. Sermons and other nonfiction prose works disappear entirely. While *Harper* is a particularly extreme example, similar things could be said about the anthologies produced by Norton and D. C. Heath.[1] Implicitly, the narrative movement of the anthologies suggests with Matthew Arnold that Literature has come to replace Religion as the central cultural achievement of the West. As well-worn as this trope is, it surely continues to animate the production of American literature anthologies and continues to affect other institutional manifestations of literary study.

But the analogy is unstable. For instance, the argument that fictional or poetic literature is the central cultural achievement of Americans weakens when the significance of John Barth's fiction is compared to that of the sermons of Martin Luther King Jr. or the politico-religious speeches of Malcolm X, or even to the editorial writings of someone like Reinhold Niebuhr. While Barth is read by a few hundred English teachers and their long-suffering students, the work of these religious and ethnic Americans has shaped the ethical, political, and imaginative practice of millions and continues to do so.

Of course, influence is not everything. But even if we apply traditional criteria of aesthetic distinction, it seems clear that the rhetoric of King, Malcolm X, or Niebuhr is of the first rank. Apparently, then, the anthologies assume their work is not literature because it is something else: nonfiction, sermonic, religious, political. But by this generic standard most of what is now considered the literature of the colonial and early national periods would be excluded as well, as would be much of Emerson, Fuller, and Thoreau. The result is the curious argument that we consider certain generic forms literary in an early period because they were culturally significant, but we now consider other forms literary even though few people in our culture bother reading them.

This shift toward an esoteric rather than an inclusive definition of literature is reflected in the tools with which we read. Even if one agreed that anthologies of the modern period should only include fiction and poetry, it remains perplexing that religious practice and tradition should remain so small a part of the context in which literature is discussed. For instance, in the *Columbia Literary History of the United States,* Charles Molesworth introduces the social context of postwar literature saying, "Most of the political and social history of post war America takes place in the context of two overwhelming developments: the international leadership of America in terms of global strategy and economic development for Western nations, and the gradual but seemingly inevitable growth of post-industrial society" (1023).

This thesis has the useful and self-evident ring that one might expect from a general reference. Clearly the global leadership of the United States and the growth of postindustrial society have been determinatively important. However, in a long and otherwise insightful overview, Molesworth does not mention religion as even a minor feature of the postwar context. This absence is striking given the degree to which religions continue to motivate cultural action around the globe. While the postwar period is often characterized as that in which the liberal Protestant consensus was finally fracturing, we might better say that the period has been characterized by the proliferation of new and more vigorous, more public, and more political religious practice. The dominance of Jewish writers in the postwar period sprang from the influx of Jewish immigrants in the pre- and postwar periods and from the development of a newly assertive intellectual and religious community. Carol Kessner has pointed out that despite the tendency to view secular "New York Intellectuals" as the norm, Jewish American culture in the twentieth century has produced a number of powerful intellectuals and writers who wished to remain closely connected to various forms of Judaism. The Native American literary renaissance is connected to a revival of Native American religious practice. The bland but well-meaning political passivity of liberal white congregations gave way before the politico-religious flood tide of the Civil Rights and Black Power movements—a fact which, when ignored, makes many concerns of both John Updike and Amiri Baraka uninterpretable. It is difficult to see how a critic or teacher can engage the black arts movement or its cultural descendants like rap without some engagement with the development of pan-African religions and the growth of Islam as a religious force in the inner cities.

With Robert Bellah, one could also note that the countercultural movements of the sixties bore all the characteristics of American revivalism even if they were not specifically Christian. While some of these movements were escapist, they often resulted in a politically engaged call for a redeemed society in the tradition of the American Jeremiad (*Beyond* xvii–xviii, cited in May 17). Moreover, some sixty million Americans of all races and both genders called themselves "born again" in 1992. Indeed, the dominant elements of the evangelical movement were at least partially responsible for the conservative swing in national politics that began in the 1970s and culminated in the congressional elections of 1994. Globally, the rise of Islamic nationalisms has had crucial political ramifications, to say nothing of literary ramifications as witnessed in the agony of Salman Rushdie under threat of the recently lifted *fatwa*.

None of these developments emerge or could even be guessed at in what is now perhaps the standard reference work by which harried scholars and teachers, preparing for undergraduates' surveys, will gauge the context of postwar American literature. One does not have to champion these religious movements to recognize their

importance, any more than one has to champion postindustrial capitalism in order to articulate its significance. I am not arguing here
that religious practice is really *more* central than the development of
a postindustrial society. But the absence of nearly every reference to
religious practice since 1865 suggests the degree to which the literary
profession is dependent upon Enlightenment models of securariza-
tion, and this even after Enlightenment itself has been increasingly
discredited.

These facts bespeak a situation in which most American intellectuals in the humanities have only vague, overgeneralized, or stereotypical conceptions of religious traditions and practices even while
America is the most religiously diverse and active culture in the West,
perhaps in the world. As a consequence of the marginalization of religion, contemporary scholars are able to proceed as if religious traditions have little or nothing to do with conceptions like "America,"
"ethnic," "woman," or "literature."

Religion and Literature: The Cure?

Of course, a number of critics do continue to bother with issues of
religion and literature. Indeed, in one sense, religion and literature is
a flourishing sub-industry cultivated by journals like *Christianity and
Literature*, *Religion and Literature*, *Theology and Literature*, and
Religion and the Arts. Deconstruction gave birth to a frenzy of literary/
mystical critical readings, and Harold Bloom's recent work celebrates
the Gnostic "American Religion." Indeed, such is the proliferation of
religiousness of this kind that Jonathan Culler insists that there is
not too little attention to Religion in our cultural politics, but too
much.

Nevertheless, as my reading of Benjamin's puppet suggests, religion's appearance is often a difficult and contradictory event.
Indeed, several of the major statements on religion and literature
speak eloquently about religion but at the expense of ethnic particularity. Waddling out from beneath the table, religion lives; the puppet dies.

A brief examination of several major critical/theoretical statements shows that simply celebrating religion may erase or minimize ethnicity. While Giles Gunn's *Interpretation of Otherness*,
Carol Christ's *Diving Deep and Surfacing*, and Bonnie Winsbro's

Supernatural Forces do not exhaust the varied richness of work in religion and literature, these statements have been important enough to point out a dominant tendency and suggest the need for a method that reveals both the pertinence of religion and the particularity of ethnicity.

Gunn is a justly celebrated critic of religion and culture, and his book, *The Interpretation of Otherness,* has been a well-received study of the relationship of religion and literature to what Gunn calls "the American Mind." Written in the late 1970s, his title anticipates the analysis of "Otherness" that dominated literary studies in the 1980s. However, Gunn manages to write a substantial and important book about "the American mind" without mentioning a writer of color or, for that matter, without drawing on a single writer who could not be linked to the progress of mainstream liberal Protestantism in American culture. His work is dominated by Stowe, Melville, Twain, Dickinson, Frost, and Whitman. Provocative writers all, but an exclusive list. In part, the absence of ethnic authors could be chalked up to the traditional arguments concerning the exclusivity of an ethnocentric canon. However, for my purposes I am interested in the way that Gunn's understanding of religion leads him almost inexorably to discount those writers who might give a different cast or coloration to the American mind.

Describing his understanding of religion, Gunn say, "[The] function of religion is to restore our confidence in the world, in the reality and final worth of our existence, and to help us bear up in the face of life's numerous challenges and obstacles" (108). For Gunn, this characterization of religion's edifying effects soon implies the irrelevance of specific religious histories and cultures.

> [This] does not rule out the fact that most religious people have often believed or felt something a good deal more specific than this general conviction about the relationship between one's values and the inherent structure of reality. It simply assumes (and, I think, can quite readily show) that any more specific set of beliefs . . . are but individual variants of this more basic conviction. And, viewing them as such, it thus allows us to consider as at least potentially religious a great variety of ideas, actions, feelings, and so forth, that make no explicit reference either to divine beings, sacred rites, ecclesiastical institutions, or confessional traditions. (110)

Talal Asad has pointed out that by emphasizing religious practices as symbolic structures rather than embodied cultural practices, the anthropologist focuses on religion as a system of discursive beliefs about a "more basic reality" (27–54). As belief, religion becomes an individualized, psychological phenomenon, one for which specific cultural practices may provide a matrix but for which they are substantively unimportant. Since religion is everywhere essentially the same, the particularities of community and tradition are less important than the realities to which they speak and could, in practice, be roadblocks to more substantive understanding.[2]

Gunn's language replicates this anthropological imperialism almost without exception, and the result is a fundamentally psychological understanding of religion. One no longer need make "explicit reference either to divine beings, sacred rites, ecclesiastical institutions or confessional traditions" (110). Throughout most of his work, Gunn follows his theory and indeed makes few references to any specific religious traditions at all, relying instead on an abstract cultural psychology that he calls "the American Mind." Given this a-cultural and individualistic view of religion, it is unsurprising that Gunn relies on writers most sympathetic to the impulses of Protestantism on the American scene and excludes those writers who might be seen as drawing from religious traditions that promote communal solidarity such as can be found among a wide variety of American ethnic groups.[3]

In *Diving Deep and Surfacing,* Carol Christ is less interested in tracing the contours of a monumental "American Mind" and is more attuned to the ways in which women have found in religion an important resource for discovering new identities and resisting oppression. For these reasons her work provides a useful corrective to Gunn. Like Gunn, however, Christ seems mostly disinterested in or unaware of the powerful presence of ethnic women in literature, including only a single chapter on Notzake Shange. Somewhat apologetically in the introduction to the second edition, Christ generously notes that she has been too universalizing in her approach and that if she were beginning the book again she would be more cognizant of the work of women of color (xii).

However, given her theory of religion and spirituality, it is hard to see what substantive significance ethnic women, their histories, or their traditions possibly could have to her study. Christ defines religion and spirituality "in a way that enables women to recognize the spiritual in all areas of their lives, not simply in relation to the institutional church or synagogue" (xvii). Indeed, cultural practices cannot be reduced to their institutional manifestations. As I will suggest later in this chapter, many of the writers I investigate have a difficult relationship with their traditions, not least because these institutions often have been shaped by patriarchy. Nevertheless, for Christ, "recognizing the spiritual in all areas" of life becomes primarily a process that dislodges women from traditional cultural practices in the name of a more authentic, individualized, and feminine spirituality.

For instance, Christ argues that her students' religious experiences can be understood in relationship to Persephone, Demeter, and Artemis. Her courses end with each woman contributing to a class ritual in the building of an altar and, in some cases, developing rituals of her own. Whatever their psychological or spiritual significance, one wonders how an African American woman will better understand the ecstasy of the holiness shout by referencing Persephone and Demeter rather than the holiness or Pentecostal traditions of the black church or by delving even further to the roots of the shout in African religions. Nor is it clear that a Jewish American woman recognizes her identity more clearly in the fertility goddesses of Greece and Rome or that Persephone could adequately symbolize the significance of the Pueblo Its'y'ity'i, as if the specificity of geography were really substantively unimportant. Indeed, in her reading of Shange, one is hard pressed to find any significance in the black church, in alternative folk traditions, or even in newly invented Pan-African religions. Even if Shange rejects all those things, that is surely significant and says something about her self-conception as an African American woman. The "vision of women's culture" that Christ calls for in her conclusion does not seem to allow for this multiplicity (119), and her method comes too close to replicating in the name of "Women's Spirituality" what Gunn accomplishes in the name of "The American Mind."

In comparison to the synthesizing efforts of Christ and Gunn, Bonnie Winsbro's *Supernatural Forces* foregrounds the distinctive visions and practices of ethnic religious traditions and sees such traditions as responding to the political and social conditions in which they are embedded. Indeed, in Winsbro's subtitle, "*Belief, Difference, and Power in Contemporary Works by Ethnic Women,"* the categories of difference and power indicate the degree to which ethnic traditions resist the homogenizing and functionalist strategies of writers like Gunn and Christ.

"Belief" is more problematic. As I noted above, modern attempts to categorize and delimit religious experiences have tended to valorize "belief" as a universalizing category. Similarly, due to her emphasis on "belief," Winsbro constantly verges on Protestantizing her subject of investigation, as is evident in her overriding concern with "individuation" in the work of ethnic women. She says,

> Taken together, these works argue that the survival and growth of ethnic individuals depend on effective self-definition, the process by which they define who they are and what they believe in relation to surrounding social units—family, community/tribe, and society at large. Such an experience of individuation, if completed successfully, instills personal power, a power that in some cases is supplemented by a belief in an alternative reality, one that acknowledges the existence of those spirits, deities, and empowered humans who are celebrated and remembered in culturally specific folklore, myths, and religion. (6)

Interesting in this construction is the individual seeking personal power who is "surrounded" by family, community, and society. Rather than having one's individuality grounded in practices of the community, the individual knows herself in opposition to the collective.[4] Winsbro hints at this opposition in the threatening connotations of being "surrounded." The implications of this opposition blossom as her theoretical introduction proceeds. The individual must proceed in the effort of "self-definition" through "the construction of one's own world and one's own identity, for the location and claiming of one's own center" (6).

As I noted above, it is surely the case that women have needed to engage their traditions in a critical manner. But in emphasizing this as an individualizing process, Winsbro tends to acknowledge tradition while emphasizing individual psychology. In her reading of Louise Erdrich's *Tracks,* she makes no distinction between the starkly different responses of Fleur, Pauline, and Nanapush to the incursions of modernity because each response is individually empowering. Pauline's peculiar and self-destructive form of Catholicism—

characterized by the excision of cultural memory—is no different from Nanapush's creative effort to continue cultural memories on a new basis for the sake of the tribe. Similarly, Winsbro's emphasis on Tayo's problem of "belief" in Silko's *Ceremony* turns a cultural drama into a drama of individual conversion and salvation. Tayo's sexual encounters with Night Swan and Ts'eh and his participation in Betonie's sand painting ceremony merely illustrate things he ought to believe. Thus Winsbro downplays their significance as acts of a community rather than of an individual. Her characters sound like troubled Euro-American Protestants rather than individuals shaped by unique cultural traditions. To this degree, at least, Winsbro's readings verge too close to the homogenizing tendencies evident in her scholarly precursors, Christ and Gunn.

Religion, Counter-memory, and Community

The foregoing discussion suggests that the institutions of literary studies have had a difficult time with the specificity of ethnic religious traditions. I am letting pass without discussion the critically difficult issue of how religion remains mute in the literature classroom—the primary space of literary study. On the one hand, the dominant strains of the literary academy have done little to promote or even provide a coherent description of religion at all, as is evident in the dominant anthologies, commentaries, and literary theories. Religion remains securely beneath the table. On the other hand, when scholars concerned with religion and literature do begin to discuss religion, ethnicity disappears in favor of the religious "universal."

Without imagining that the task is easy, it has seemed to me that one way to thread a route past the Scylla of silence and the Charybdis of universalism is to foreground religions as forms of cultural memory. Peter Berger has pointed out that one of the founding elements of any social world is shared memory, going so far as to say that "society, in its essence, is a memory" (41). Berger locates the socially constructive power of religion not so much in doctrines or theologies but in day-to-day practices, stories, and rituals: ways of being in the world imaginatively and practically that orient human beings toward particular forms of action. The stories and rituals that religions carry forward embody memories that allow cultures to both persist and adapt to change.

Men forget. They must, therefore, be reminded over and over again.
. . . Religious ritual has been a crucial instrument of this process of
"reminding." Again and again it "makes present" to those who participate in it the fundamental reality-definitions and their appropriate legitimations. . . . Both religious acts and religious legitimations, ritual and
mythology, *dromena* and *legoumena, together* serve to "recall" the traditional meanings embodied in the culture and its major institutions.
They restore ever again the continuity between the present moment and
the societal tradition, placing the experiences of the individual and the
various groups of the society in the context of a history (fictitious or not)
that transcends them all. (40–41)

While Berger at times verges toward the same universalizing that I
have critiqued in Gunn and Christ, his emphasis on memory rescues
the specific character of religious traditions and their narratives.
Narrative exists nowhere except in the detail of its telling and retelling.
Thus, cultural memories are nonessentializing and emphasize the possibility of collective action while not neglecting the incorporation of
individual experience. They embody and produce different forms of
social and historical consciousness. Moreover, such memories take the
multiple and diverse forms of narrative itself. Given this historical
specificity, the unique narratives upon which groups draw must be
examined in detail and with a consciousness of distinction, rather than
reducing them to symbolic manifestations of "The American Mind,"
"Women's Spirituality," or even "Ethnicity."

As a polyvocal narrative form, fiction—or in Maxine Hong
Kingston's case, fictionalized memoir—can textualize the ethnic cultural memories that are elsewhere ritualized, embodied, disciplined,
and maintained through religious traditions. Fictions provide a discursive space wherein the counter-memories of ethnic religious practices
can be articulated and can resist the universalizing and rationalizing
impulse of enlightenment.[5] Thus, many ethnic women writers have
drawn on the specificity of their cultural memories—embodied in ritual or other religious practices—in order to address the forgetfulness
of ethnicity that has seemed endemic to American culture until quite
recently. For instance, by organizing her novel *Ceremony* around a
number of Pueblo stories concerning the creation of the earth and the
emergence of the Pueblo people, Silko is able to revivify a cultural
tradition in a new milieu and for a new cultural period. Similarly,
Cynthia Ozick attempts to address the fragmentation of Jewish

culture under the pressure of both the Holocaust and assimilation by incorporating narratives, themes, and images from Jewish history and legal commentary.

By drawing on the resiliency of religious traditions, such writers resist or transform dominant ideologies and contribute to the maintenance of the religious communities in which they participate. As I suggested above, the cultural memories embodied in religions have sustained ethnic groups even while these groups sustain those memories. Examining ethnic religious traditions, we see not so much the quest for individual self-realization as the social process of world-building. African American Christianity in the United States is not so much a private practice as the focus of community life, politics, culture, education, and spirituality to such a degree that it would be impossible to point to a specifiable "religious" element separable from all these other practices (Frazier 35–51; Lincoln 155–56). Reservations have, in some instances, given Native Americans space in which traditional Indian forms of life may be practiced and altered to inform new historical situations. Though rarely remembered now, the United Farm Workers' movement led by Cesar Chavez had a significant religious motivation and justification, as was evidenced in the predominant and pervasive symbol of the Virgin of Guadalupe. More recently, the rebellion of Chiapas peasants in Mexico has been at least partly the result of base community work among the peasants by radical Roman Catholic priests.

Thus, many stories of many ethnic women writers are about the possibility of life together. How and where this happens varies immensely, dependent as these communities are upon the various imaginations available through traditional religions and the different ways in which those religions address contemporary concerns. In *The Color Purple* Alice Walker begins with an emphasis on the Christianity common to most African American women but, finding it inadequate, develops a more pantheistic vision in sympathy with African religions. The community that develops is first primarily a community of women and then a hybrid community that contains both men and women shaped by African and Christian stories. While it is at some remove from the traditional black Baptist church, the community of *The Color Purple* remains in a recognizably Afro-Christian tradition in its combination of African, Christian, and modern Western modes of thought and behavior. Similarly, in *Woman*

Warrior, Kingston attempts to delineate the complex identity of a self in relationship to both the ancestral past, the familial present, and the social context of her everyday life. The result is a hybrid form that honors her relationship to women in her past while also emphasizing her uniqueness in the present.

My emphases thus far suggest that cultural memory is not static and unchanging and that literature is part of the process of registering and creating this change. My emphasis on the changing quality of memory is crucial if we are to see religious traditions as effective resources for imagining cultural change. The simple and unassailable fact is that religious traditions of every stripe have been irrevocably altered by contact with modern science, capitalism or communism, ideologies of the independent individual, and the technologies of print and electronics. To ignore such "facts on the ground" would dematerialize ethnic religions, playing quite easily into many traditional assumptions concerning ethnic religion. Indeed, modernity has often "forgotten" such traditions by assigning them to a misty prehistory that is no longer applicable to the present. Cordelia Candelaria has pointed out that a consistent trope in America literature from Natty Bumppo to Huckleberry Finn has been an idealization of ethnicity as a special locus of community; this community, however, exists primarily in a utopian space outside of history or is associated with the mists of the distant past. Just as Chingachgook, the Noble Savage of James Fenimore Cooper's imagination, passes away into the past we long for nostalgically, many investigations of both ethnicity and religion have tended to emphasize their unchanging attachment to past cultural forms.

But the quality of cultural memory is such that its applicability is new in every act of remembrance, precisely because the context in which memory occurs is new. Thus, the dimensions of memory are, at least potentially, constantly refreshed and changed. Similarly, the content of cultural memory changes as new memories are added to the cultural stories. For example, the memory of Christopher Columbus is different in the 1990s because it has been complicated by the renewed memory of Native American cultures. Conversely, the cultural memories of various tribes have been altered by the fact of European contact and culture. In another instance, we can point out that memories of the Pueblo past do not exist in a static and unchanging way but take on new resonances as they are woven together with new Pueblo memories that have imbibed some of the values of modernity. Speaking of her own practice as a writer, Silko says,

> I write [traditional Laguna stories] down because I like seeing how I can translate this sort of feeling or flavor or sense of a story that's told and heard onto the page. Obviously, some things will be lost because you're going from one medium to another. And I use translate in the broadest sense. I don't mean translate from the Laguna Pueblo language to English, I mean the feeling or the sense that language is being used orally. . . . I recognize the inherent problem; there's no way that hearing a story and reading a story are the same thing; but that doesn't mean that everyone should throw up his hands and say it can't be done or say that what's done on the page isn't catching some of those senses. (Barnes 50–51)

Essentially, Silko is speaking of a process of hybridizing whereby the original cultural location of stories is incorporated into a new cultural form. This does not mean that past meanings have disappeared, but that they have a more complicated resonance for contemporary American culture and for tribal cultures than they had in the past. This resonance makes them available for the present in fundamentally new ways. The meanings of the past are relived and rearticulated to make them available and useful for the present.

Homi Bhabha has pointed out that this process of hybridization transforms culture. In this transformation, the forms of dominant cultural authority are inhabited in such a way as to become "virtually unrecognizable" to their original producers as "the knowledges of cultural authority" are transformed by their "[articulation] with the forms of 'native' knowledges" (115). Put another way for my purposes, we could say that the process by which ethnic religious traditions ("native knowledges") incorporate the forms and processes of contemporary culture in the United States is unpredictable and the result is a hybrid form. Traditional cultural memories take on new resonances in new contexts, and new forms of social solidarity or communal alliance are enabled, given the new stories that are being told.

Conceived of as a hybrid practice, then, the communities envisioned by ethnic authors need not belong simply to the misty past but can be seen as forms of social solidarity adapted to the present. This is not to say that these writers are never subject to nostalgic utopianism. However, the writers I am examining are characterized by a more active engagement of past with present and vice versa. For example, in *Ceremony,* Leslie Silko envisions viable Pueblo traditions as continuing into the present by incorporating elements of contemporary culture and elements of other native traditions.

The tension between innovation and tradition inherent in this process points to my focus on the unique role of women writers. In general I agree with Bonnie Winsbro when she asserts that women writers evince a particularly pronounced concern with issues of religion, community, and cultural memory, though she does not explain fully why this might be the case, nor is she able to account for those male writers who evince similar concerns (11–12). More to the point than religious or communitarian themes in the work of women writers is the particularly difficult location of ethnic women's culture, a location in which the competing claims of modernity and tradition are brought to bear with a unique force. On the one hand, women's roles have been structured culturally so as to posit women as guardians of religion and tradition. On the other hand, those same traditions have often reinforced destructive practices toward women, practices that have, in part, been alleviated by a modern discourse of individuals' rights and justice. The force of these two competing structures encourages women to seek a reconciliation between tradition and modern forms of cultural life.

Since at least the nineteenth century, women have been cast as the particular guardians of religion, community, and cultural memory. The private/public split that placed white American women in the home emphasized the woman's role within the family, the church, the friendships of society, none of which was separable from some identifiable inward "religious" element but was warp and woof of what it meant to be a Christian in the nineteenth century.[6] Harriet Beecher Stowe envisions the possibility of a just and Christian society, writing *Uncle Tom's Cabin* as an explicitly religio-political protest of the institution of slavery. Women's groups worked for the vote out of a sense of religious commitment, and temperance leagues invoked the language of the churches in an effort to define appropriate community behavior. Paul Gutjahr has suggested that one mark of the spiritual superiority of Jesus in the nineteenth century lay in his apparently feminine characteristics, important to a century that believed in the "more biologically sensitive, thus more religious attuned, bodies of women" (162). Indeed, the dominance of women in all such "cultural" areas of life led Ann Douglas to write her persuasive account of the "feminization of American culture." While we cannot discount the immense changes of the twentieth century, this narrative in which women are the guardians of culture and tradition while men are the guardians of everything else still has a deeply felt emotional appeal, as is surely evident not only in pews on Sunday morning but also in the large numbers of women who fill out the undergraduate classroom in literature and other fine arts or humanities disciplines.

While the situation of ethnic women has not mirrored this structure precisely—for one thing ethnic women in many instances have not had the luxury of occupying the home to the exclusion of work outside the home—the symbolic weight of the structure is powerful. It has had an enduring appeal as an ideal and has partially shaped the role ethnic women occupy with regard to religion in their own social locations. The writers I investigate are inheritors of this cultural construct, but they also write with a sensitivity to the limitations of such constructs, to say nothing of the limitations of their traditions. While domestic religion and literary activity have been particularly important locations for women's "public" activity, the consequences for women simply cannot be ignored. Among other things, this conception of religion and community potentially feeds the destructive ideology that a woman's "place" is to lose her identity in the nurturing of others, whether those others are men, children, or the community at large. Indeed, one of the great novels of the past two decades, Toni Morrison's *Beloved,* is concerned with the destructive possibilities inherent within the woman's role as one who exists "for others."

Further, while I have been insisting on the cultural viability of religious traditions and their memories, even the most cursory historical investigation uncovers the brutal fact of religious justification for violence against women. Memories are often memories of pain. Ethnic religious traditions have not been exempt from this tendency, as is made graphically clear by both Walker's representation of African American Christianity and Kingston's representation of the consequences of Chinese traditions. Even Leslie Silko, who suggests that oppression of women has not been characteristic of native traditions, recognizes that, in practice, tribes have been affected by their contact with European models of gender roles.[7]

Thus in this book I examine women writers not simply because I see them as more interested in religion than men. Such a construct always begs the question of the exception. Rather, women write from a particular location that accentuates the problem of trying to maintain a tradition in the contemporary world, in part because that world sometimes offers resources for women's self-realization that traditions may not. Were religious traditions simply static, then the only alternative open to women would be acquiescence—accepting life as ordained by God or the gods—or abandonment of tradition in favor of the manifest freedoms of individual liberty. If, however, religious traditions are understood as hybrid forms, then these women may approach the memories carried by tradition differently. They are traditions that must be understood differently given the new context of the group. Part of that new context includes changed gender relationships.

Part of the project that these writers undertake, then, is a process of reenvisioning their traditions, or re-membering them differently. Speaking of this process, Adrienne Rich says the following:

> Re-vision—the act of looking back, of seeing with fresh eyes, of entering an old text from a new critical direction—is for us more than a chapter in cultural history: it is an act of survival. Until we can understand the assumptions in which we are drenched we cannot know ourselves. And this drive to self-knowledge, for woman, is more than a search for identity: it is part of her refusal of the self-destructiveness of male-dominated society. A radical critique of literature, feminist in its impulse, would take the work first of all as a clue to how we live, how we have been living, how we have been led to imagine ourselves, how our language has trapped as well as liberated us; and how we can begin to see—and therefore live—afresh. (90)

Rich's notion of re-vision suggests neither abandonment nor acquiescence. This is doubly important for the work of ethnic women who neither abandon modernity nor acquiesce to it, who neither abandon traditions nor acquiesce to patriarchal or otherwise destructive elements of their traditions. For instance, Ana Castillo has remarked that it is impossible to excise Catholicism from the experience of Mexican Americans without destroying the culture, but that Catholicism must be reenvisioned to emphasize its possibilities for women (*Massacre* 95–96). Similarly, Ozick insists on the centrality of

Judaism to Jewish identity, despite its patriarchal history. Simply by casting herself as a commentator on the tradition, Ozick refuses the community's exclusion of Jewish women from access to the law. Kingston draws on traditions of ancestor remembrance to remember female ancestors previously excised or made marginal to the culture's memory.

Drawing on and revising Raymond Williams, we might say then that religions in these works by ethnic women are both residual and emergent formations.[8] Because they draw on the past and envision past values and forms of life in their work, women use the residue of the past as a means of articulating the present. However, because they reenvision this past, they rearticulate it through engagement with the present in its manifold change and pressure toward the future. Because they recognize the limitations of the past and attempt to reimagine them for a possible life in the present, they also represent an emergent response to the sexism and ethnic oppression that continue to exist in the present. Any critical reading that seeks to do justice to the particular modes by which ethnic women have engaged religion must account for this creative tension between past and present which results in new cultural memories for the future.

2

Disruptive Memories

CYNTHIA OZICK AND THE INVENTED PAST

> *He that applieth himself to the fear of God,*
> *And setteth his mind upon the Law of the Most High,*
> *He searcheth out the wisdom of all the ancients,*
> *And is occupied with the prophets of old.*
> —The Wisdom of Ben Sira

*T*he tension between tradition and modernity that I outlined in the last chapter has long been a crucial theme in ethnic literature, often expressing itself in a tension between the desire for assimilation and the desire for family connection. For instance, midway through *Bread Givers,* Anzia Yezierska's novel of immigrant experience, young Sara Smolinsky confronts her father, who represents Old World Judaism:

> Wild with all that was choked in me since I was born, my eyes burned into my father's eyes. "My will is as strong as yours. I'm going to live my own life. Nobody can stop me. I'm not from the old country. I'm American!"
>
> "You blasphemer!" His hand flung out and struck my cheek. "Denier of God! I'll teach you respect for the law!"
>
> I leaped back and dashed for the door. The Old World had struck its last on me. (138)

This moment capsulizes the great themes of immigrant Jewish novelists such as Yezierska, Mary Antin, and Abraham Cahan. Sara Smolinsky's denial of her father and his cultural memories is the necessary breach through which she casts herself into Americanness, a blasphemy by which she gains her life. As the novel progresses, Sara does gain her life, not through placement in a religious cosmos or by inheriting religious memory but through education and success in a chosen profession. By the end of the novel, American life has broken the father's body if not his will, and his dependence on Sara for food and shelter suggests the ultimate triumph of assimilation over a fractured traditionalism.

This narrative anticipates the dominant image of Jewish American culture among writers and academics. Irving Howe's *World of Our Fathers* is a monumental work of cultural history; it also eulogizes the loss of a Jewish tradition that has not been maintained in the United States. The best known and most honored Jewish author in America, Philip Roth, writes about being a Jew who has no substantive Jewish identity. Indeed Roth's most anthologized short story eerily redraws Yezierska's scene of religious violence. In "The Conversion of the Jews," young Ozzie Freedman corners his rabbi in a debate about the transcendent powers of God. When the rabbi relies on sarcasm and humiliation, Ozzie lashes out:

> "You don't know! You don't know anything about God!"
>
> The rabbi spun back towards Ozzie. "What?"
>
> "You don't know—you don't—"
>
> "Apologize, Oscar, apologize!" It was a threat.
>
> "You don't—"
>
> Rabbi Binder's hand flicked out at Ozzie's cheek. Perhaps it had only been meant to clamp the boy's mouth shut, but Ozzie ducked and the palm caught him squarely on the nose.
>
> The blood came in a short, red spurt onto Ozzie's shirt front.
>
> The next moment was all confusion. Ozzie screamed, "You bastard, you bastard!" and broke for the classroom door. (146–47)

As with Yezierska, Roth represents religious tradition as that force which clamps shut the questioning mouth of freedom. Judaism's bastardy is clearest in its inability to use language convincingly without the underpinnings of communal censure.

This myth of escape from the ethnic and religious enclave into the light of America is not unique to Jewish Americans, but it bears peculiar force since such escape seems everywhere to have become fact. The successes of Jewish writers in the fifties and sixties once led John Updike to a sustained fret over the popularity of things ethnic in American literature.[1] While Updike's paranoia about his unmarketable ethnicity has abated, the importance of Jewish writers certainly has not. The academic and popular recognition of writers like Roth, Bellow, I. B. Singer, Robert Pinsky, Alicia Ostriker, Louis Simpson, Adrienne Rich, or more recently of Allegra Goodman and Nathan Englander, indeed even of Cythia Ozick herself, testifies to the continuing significance of Jewish American culture to the American scene as a whole. Such success reflects the larger cultural movement of Jewish Americans into the mainstream of American economic, social, academic, and political life.[2] With the vast majority of Jewish Americans, Jewish writers have made the exodus out of the metaphorical ghetto and into the promised land of the white American mainstream.

Cynthia Ozick reads and participates in this journey with a furrowed brow and a searching glance into the past. At the extreme, she believes that some American writers have exchanged the promises of God for the more comforting fleshpots of Egypt, or in this case America. The exodus into the suburbs seems to signal the end of Jewish tradition as a coherent moment in human history: "To be a Jew is to be old in history, but not only that; to be a Jew is to be a member of a distinct civilization expressed through an oceanic culture in possession of a group of essential concepts and a multitude of texts and attitudes elucidating those concepts. Next to the density of such a condition—or possibility—how gossamer are the stories of those writers 'of Jewish extraction' whose characters are pale indifferent echoes of whatever lies at hand: this or that popular impingement" (*Metaphor* 224).

For Ozick, the success of Philip and Henry Roth, Norman Mailer, and others is achieved by exchanging Jewish ethical and religious ideals for italicized Yiddish phrases, chicken soup, and jokes about Jewish mothers. Consequently, Jewish memory is no longer an effective cultural force.[3]

Against this tendency, Ozick remains committed to the central traditions of Jewish religious thought and practice.[4] Wielding an iconoclastic club against Harold Bloom's Oedipal theories of culture, Ozick affirms the following: "[Jewish liturgy] posits *recapturing without revision* the precursor's stance and strength when it iterates 'our God, and God of our fathers, God of Abraham, Isaac, and Jacob.' Nearly every congeries of Jewish thought is utterly set against the idea of displacing the precursor. 'Torah' includes the meanings of *tradition* and *transmittal* together" (*Ardor* 194).

This attention to tradition suggests that cultural memory embodied in religious practice is the focal point of Jewish identity. Historiographer Yerushalmi has suggested that for Jewish religious thought, "God reveals himself in the course of [history]. . . . Far from attempting a flight from history, biblical religion allows itself to be saturated by it and is inconceivable apart from it" (9). Similarly, Ozick notes that the ethics of everyday life are based upon cultural memory, upon remembering what God has done for the people of Israel and applying that memory to relations with others (*Metaphor* 279). The persistence of a Jewish life is dependent upon millennia of Jewish memories. Thus, Elaine Kauvar rightly asserts that for Ozick "the principle of continuity overwhelmingly takes precedence over the desire to create new forms" (xii).

Still, if cultural memory is at the root of Jewish life, recent history has threatened the continuity of that memory. Jewish memory has faced at least two fundamental threats to its continuity and integrity: assimilation and the Holocaust. Motivated by the crisis these events precipitate, Ozick attempts to re-create collective memories through fiction. She addresses this crisis of memory as she forges a fiction at once contemporary and memorial, in keeping with the history of Jewish religious practice.

Assimilation and the Isolated Jew

Guarding against "assimilation" has been a constitutive feature of Jewish religious practice since Moses, as is evidenced by injunctions against idolatry and against intermarriage.[5] Yet this injunction takes on peculiar and ambiguous force in the modern period, when, after centuries of persecution and enforced separation at the hands of the church, the Jews of Europe were "invited" to join what Benedict Anderson describes as the "imagined community" of the nation-state. Anderson's work brilliantly analyzes the ways in which cultural institutions, including literature, go about shaping the imagination of this new community, but he does less to help us understand what happens to religious traditions as they take their place within this new imaginative order. As I suggested in my first chapter, cultural institutions have domesticated and individualized religious belief at the expense of collective memories and practices. Thus, the emancipatory rhetoric of modernity is highly ambiguous. On the one hand, the Napoleonic concords effectively freed Jews from legal and political restrictions that had been in place through the centuries of Christendom. Who could doubt that this development is preferable to pogroms and enforced separateness? On the other hand, this equality has been purchased at the price of distinctiveness. The Jew could be a citizen, but only by keeping her Jewishness at home and under wraps (Arthur Cohen 12ff). To some degree these developments encouraged a new assertiveness on the part of Jewish women as modern forms of Judaism gradually encouraged the participation of women in worship and study. But this participation did not challenge a basic structure that diminished Judaism as an explanatory cultural narrative, nor did it radically challenge or change the notion of the home as the woman's proper sphere. *Haskalah*—the term for the Jewish Enlightenment— rang with the good intentions of Enlightenment universalism, but in practice it reduced Judaism's relevance to daily life. As a result, Judaism was displaced as the central and necessary feature of Jewish life in Western societies.

This displacement has been particularly noticeable in the United States. With near unanimity, historians, sociologists, and religious philosophers perceive a state of crisis in the Jewish American community, a crisis precipitated by the loss of specific Jewish memories, beliefs, and practices. In a harsh assessment, Arthur Cohen suggests that "In the last fifty years, the uninformed, the religiously illiterate, and the socially assimilated have succeeded in affecting, if not shaping, the religion offered by the synagogue. Judaism is more than ever a reaction to the disinterest and embarrassment of the already secularized Jewish majority. . . . [The] Jew has become, in matters Jewish, doggedly and uncritically American" (191).

While disgust colors Cohen's assessment, other scholars affirm his thesis. Arthur Hertzberg notes that the Jewish "conquest of the suburbs" in the 1950s trivialized Jewish religious life. According to Hertzberg, some 70 percent of all American Jews maintained a general belief in God, but synagogue life reflected the respectable religiosity of mainline American Protantism in the 1950s (327–30).

Nathan Glazer suggests that "Few Jews would know what the principles of the Jewish faith are" (130). Ozick summarizes the tone and content of postwar Jewish American scholarship when she says, "An understanding of the unique content of Jewish genius has been forfeited by the great majority of modern Jews. It is the Enlightenment that has made us forfeit the understanding and forget the content" (*Metaphor* 232).

Ozick reads the literature "of Jewish extraction" as one index of this forgetfulness. Nevertheless, the prevalence of such literature points out a significant problem in Ozick's call for a literature of "transmission and transmittal": Ozick cannot be certain of a common ground with her audience. If no community of memory exists, how may memories be evoked or transmitted at all? Historiographer Yerushalmi delineates this problem further: "The collective memories of the Jewish people were a function of the shared faith, cohesiveness, and will of the group itself. . . . The decline of Jewish collective memory in modern times is only a symptom of the unraveling of that common network of belief and praxis through whose mechanisms . . . the past was once made present. Therein lies the root of the malady. Ultimately Jewish memory cannot be 'healed' or rejuvenated" (94).

I will return to question Yerushalmi's forbidding diagnosis. However, to the degree that it must be endorsed, it creates some difficult conundrums for Ozick's aesthetics of memory. Once lived participation in cultural memory is fragmented, memory cannot be reinstated by fiat. Thus, Ozick may speak in a vacuum if memories are as broken and fragmentary as Ozick and many others seem to think. Rather than writing out of a sense of collective memory and historical depth, perhaps Ozick will only be writing to isolated American citizens whose ancestry happens to be Jewish.

Who can evoke memory if memory is lost? The strain of this impossibility forces Ozick to re-create the past as invention. In her work, memory tends to disturb the placid surface of the everyday, serving as a cautionary mechanism and as a means of renewing cultural memory.

Throughout Ozick's fiction, the disturbing past appears in fantastic guise to warn against forgetfulness or to provide some fragmentary instruction about the past. Ruth Puttermesser, a character to whom Ozick has returned in several stories, is in need of such cautionary reminders. Puttermesser is in search of history, a living connection to the past that will give her life meaning beyond her mundane efforts in a civic bureaucracy. In "Puttermesser: Her Work History, Her Ancestry, Her Afterlife," Puttermesser is starkly and plainly a solitary. At thirty-four she is single and living alone. She is the only Jewish woman in the law firm which she eventually leaves. Even though there are other Jewish lawyers in the firm who also eventually leave, gender conventions separate her from them and their male activities. She has no friends worth mentioning, and she spends her free time playing chess against herself or completing crossword puzzles from the *New York Times*. Her parents have retired to Florida. She is without connection, and particularly without connection to a living Jewish community of memory.

To some degree, Puttermesser is aware of her ethnicity. She is aware of ethnic markers such as the appearance of her face and the linguistic differences between Jews and Gentiles in the office. Moreover, she makes some effort to learn Hebrew grammar, and the references to the Dreyfus affair in the story suggest that she has at least a cursory knowledge of Jewish history. Finally, in a letter to her mother, she evinces some concern for the plight of Soviet Jewry. By all appearances she is the model Jew without Judaism.

As industrious as much of this sounds, Puttermesser's attention to Jewish memory seems to be largely a matter of style. Ethnic markers like the sound of speech are aesthetic, not unlike the content of ethnicity that Ozick denounces in other Jewish writers. Her efforts on behalf of Soviet Jewry are mentioned only once in a context where she seems most concerned to convince her mother to stop playing matchmaker (*Levitation* 24). One must even suspect Puttermesser's attention to Hebrew grammar given the way she imagines the Hebrew verb: "The Hebrew verb, a stunning mechanism: three letters, whichever fated three, could command all possibility simply by a change in their pronunciation, or the addition of a wing-letter fore and aft. Every conceivable utterance blossomed from this trinity. It seemed to her not so much a language for expression as a code for the world's design, indissoluble, predetermined, translucent. The idea of the grammar of Hebrew turned Puttermesser's brain into a palace, a sort of Vatican; inside its corridors she walked from one resplendent triptych to another" (*Levitation* 23–24).

Joseph Lowin reads this passage as a straightforward affirmation of Hebrew's creative possibilities (131). However, the metaphorical and social context here suggests irony. To imagine the Hebrew verb as "a code for the world's design" affirms the Jewish mysticism associated with Hasidism and the Kabbalah (Scholem, *Kabbalah*, 128–44, 168–74). However, to imagine that it is not "a language for expression" cuts language off from history and community. While this mystical mode of reading resonates with kabalistic traditions taken up in other stories, the kabalistic masters saw in Torah a vast world of interconnection. Kabbalah was, finally, a way of reading that could not be separated from community and tradition. In Puttermesser's imagination, by contrast, Hebrew becomes not a vehicle for connection but a vehicle for aesthetic experience. In the Vatican of her imagination she walks alone.

Puttermesser's solitude culminates in the discussion of her Uncle Zindel. Zindel is introduced halfway through the story as, purportedly, Puttermesser's Hebrew teacher. A "former shammes in a shul that had been torn down" (*Levitation* 31), Zindel initially appears to be the necessary link to memory that Puttermesser has been missing. He is, after all, family. He is also a remnant of a coherent culture. Most significant of all, Zindel is a teacher, a man in touch with the laws, practices, and traditions of normative Judaism. As such, he both embodies the past and passes tradition on to others. One expects that Zindel will guide Puttermesser through her cultural dislocation.

But Zindel has less substance than air. Like the Vatican of Puttermesser's Hebrew, Zindel is a figment of Puttermesser's imagination: "Uncle Zindel lies under the earth of Staten Island. Puttermesser has never had a conversation with him; he died four years before her birth. He is all legend" (36). The narrative of an exiled Jew returning to her people stumbles to a halt as Ozick tells us the shammes is a sham. "Puttermesser does not remember Uncle Zindel; Puttermesser's mother does not remember him. A name in the dead grandmother's mouth. Her parents have no ancestry" (37).

Puttermesser represents the dilemma of a third generation Jewish woman whose ethnic community is threatened with dissolution under the pressures of assimilation. As the narrator suggests, "Puttermesser must claim an ancestor. She demands connection—surely a Jew must own a past. Poor Puttermesser has found herself in a world without a past" (36). The presence of Zindel as an invented memory emphasizes the absence of a viable past and serves as an index of the cultural malaise of a Jewish community without connection to history.

Indeed, if there is no connection to history, neither can there be hope for the future. Puttermesser is arrested in time.

> The scene with Uncle Zindel did not occur. It could not occur because, though Puttermesser dares to posit her ancestry, we may not. Puttermesser is not to be examined as an artifact but as an essence. Who made her? No one cares. Puttermesser is henceforth to be presented as a given. Put her back into Receipts and Disbursements, among office Jews and patronage collectors. While winter dusk blackens the Brooklyn Bridge, let us hear her opinion about the taxation of exempt properties. The bridge is not the harp Hart Crane said it was in his poem. Its staves are prison bars. . . . Hey! Puttermesser's biographer! What will you do with her now? (38)

The two short sentences "Who made her? No one cares" are damning of both Puttermesser and the Jewish community. According to covenant, God made her. To say no one cares describes a people disinterested with memory and covenant.

The reference to Hart Crane's *The Bridge* spells out the consequences of this stasis, the denial of human potential and creativity. *The Bridge* is a paean to human possibility. But, human promise is cut off in Puttermesser's world, as are individual human histories. Thus, the story ends with Ozick mocking her own enterprise. What can Puttermesser's biographer do with her now in this world without past or future, a world, in other words, with no story? The answer is nothing. While endless episodes of Puttermesser's life might be told, they are all equally insubstantial when cut off from memories which give narrative action some enduring importance.

Nevertheless, Ozick does return to Puttermesser in the novella "Puttermesser and Xanthippe." While her circumstances have changed— she has a new job and home, and she is carrying on an affair with a married man—she lives as disconnected from tradition as ever (S. Cohen 92). The affair is apparently already on the rocks at the opening of the story. Rappaport, her lover, has walked out after Puttermesser delayed his amorous advances in order to read Plato's *Theatetus*. There she reads rapturously of the philosopher's superior detachment from human events (*Levitation* 78). This detachment mirrors Puttermesser's essential detachment from the material facts of her very human life.

If anything, Puttermesser's separation from the past is more complete than in the earlier story. She lives in a garish, modern luxury apartment because her old apartment building was reduced to ashes by arsonists: "On a summer evening Puttermesser arrived home from her office without possessions: her shoes were ash, her piano teacher's penciled 'Excellent,' written in fine large letters at the top of "Humoresque" and right across the opening phrase of 'Fur Elise,' had vanished among the cinders. Puttermesser's childhood, burned away. How prescient her mother had been to take all of Puttermesser's school compositions with her to Florida! Otherwise every evidence of Puttermesser's early mental growth might have gone under in that criminal conflagration" (80).

None of these memorabilia speaks to a connection with Jewish tradition, of course. But now Puttermesser seems to live almost entirely in the present. The hopeful reference to her mother dissipates as the story proceeds. This is the mother's only "appearance" in the story.

Puttermesser's fantasy life further emphasizes her isolation. She dreams of "an ideal Civil Service: devotion to polity, the citizen's sweet love of the citizenry, the light rule of reason and common sense, the City as a miniature country crowded with patriots—not fools and jingoists, but patriots true and serene; humorous affections for the idiosyncrasies of one's distinctive little homeland, each borough itself another little homeland, joy in the Bronx, elation in Queens, O happy Richmond! Children on roller skates, and over the Brooklyn Bridge the long patchwork-colored line of joggers, breathing hard above the homeland-hugging green waters" (85). The inflated language suggests an irony that undermines such utopian aspirations. Puttermesser founds her Utopia on the rule of "reason and common sense," values associated with *haskalah*. Moreover, the possibility of a "homeland" in New York suggests she has abandoned the primary feature of the covenant's promise for the future. While Puttermesser's vision is generous, her fantasy has little to do with Jewish history or covenant.[6]

The golem legend at the center of "Puttermesser and Xanthippe" emphasizes Puttermesser's effort to gratify her immediate desires.[7] Her story contrasts starkly with that of Rabbi Judah Loew of Prague, which Puttermesser reads early in the story. Rabbi Judah Loew created a golem—a humanlike creation made of earth and brought to life through kabalistic rituals—in order to save the Jews from a pogrom carried out by Christians in an anti-Jewish hysteria. To create his golem, he "sought inner purity and sanctification by means of prayer and ritual immersion" (101). By contrast, Puttermesser creates the golem by accident. Returning home from work, she discovers a human creature shaped of clay in her bed. She circles her bed, perhaps unconsciously uttering words of unknown origin, and suddenly Xanthippe the golem lives.

If anything, the golem is produced of her desires for a daughter and for revenge on an unfair superior, not, certainly, out of desire to save the Jewish community. Early in the story, Puttermesser fantasizes a series of potential daughters: "It was self-love: all these daughters were Puttermesser as a child. She imagined a daughter in fourth grade, then in seventh grade, then in second-year high school. Puttermesser herself had gone to Hunter College High School and studied Latin" (91). Puttermesser is imagining success that many parents imagine. But her daughter will study Latin, not Hebrew or Yiddish. Rather than being connected to a community, Puttermesser is out to replicate herself, using a golem if necessary.

Although Xanthippe the golem helps establish Puttermesser's urban utopia, she also precipitates its destruction because both Xanthippe and the utopia itself are rooted in Puttermesser's self-aggrandizing imagination. Xanthippe is all appetite and so lives exclusively in the present. She cannot comprehend consequences but must only feed her growing lust for food and sex. She cannot remain loyal to her "mother," Puttermesser, since her overwhelming purpose is to fulfill her immediate desires. She grows and grows until she is finally too large to rise from the bed. She takes man after man to bed until, at last, her prolific sexuality undermines the very heaven she helped create. An image of the unbounded ego, Xanthippe ultimately threatens the well-being of her creator, Puttermesser. Self-love, this story seems to say, even in the name of the civic good, is the root of destruction.

The golem story, as well as the self-referential character of many of the other short stories, raises the thorny issue of Ozick's relationship to postmodern fictional techniques such as metafiction and magical realism. Strandberg notes that despite her dismissal of postmodernism, Ozick uses postmodern techniques as a means of breaking up the pretensions of realistic art (102). Similarly, Ellen Pifer asserts that the self-referentiality and fantasy in the Puttermesser stories emphasize that these works are fictions, creations that have no substantiality in themselves (91).

However, such readings need a supplement, in part because Ozick is a well-known champion of nineteenth-century realist novels, seeing in them the height of moral fiction. Further, iconoclasm alone does little to address Ozick's concerns with cultural memory. It seems important, then, to emphasize that Ozick's fictional world ruptures specifically at those moments when confronted with Jewish cultural memory. Uncle Zindel supplies Puttermesser's need for a past. Xanthippe embodies a medieval legend brought into the present-day political fray of New York. In "Levitation," the Jews at a party begin to levitate as a survivor of the death camps tells his tale of horror. In "Bloodshed," a Hasidic rebbe miraculously discerns a gun in the pocket of Bleilip, the assimilated Jew who is seeking some connection with the past. "Usurpation" is replete with metafictional and fantastic elements. Further, it revises another story concerning the relationship of Jewish and gentile literary traditions.

We could conclude that Jewish memory ruptures the seamless and numbing quality of American life devoted to the everyday present. Thus Norman Finkelstein's suggestion that Ozick denies historical rupture in favor of "normative patterns of belief and behavior" does not account for the tenuous character of "normative belief" in Ozick's work (73). Indeed, entirely aware of historical discontinuity, the past appears as fantastic invention, as that which is "abnormal." Ozick's work initiates rupture as much or more than it denies it.[8] Her stories are populated by people without a past who are brought into sometimes violent or disconcerting contact with embodiments of Jewish history and memory.

This clash of horizons does not always spell redemption, but it at least points out the inadequacy of lives lived without those memories. Somewhat like Flannery O'Connor, who used moments of violence to shock characters and readers into an awareness of the spiritual superficiality of American life, Ozick uses fantastic elements of Jewish memory to disrupt the ongoing patterns of the everyday.

Assimilation, Holocaust, and Re-membering

For Ozick, the dissolution of history and culture that accompanies modernity finds its most extreme expression in the Holocaust. She shares the vision of Richard Rubenstein and some of the Frankfurt School theorists who have argued that the fascist horrors are a fundamental expression of modernity, fueled in part by frustration that

Jews have not simply ceased being Jews when given the chance.[9] But perhaps more significant than its logical relationship to the dynamics of assimilation is the Holocaust's threat to Jewish memory. The Holocaust resists incorporation into the traditions of memory at the center of Judaism. Speaking of an interview with the dean of the Evangelical Church of East and West Berlin, Rubenstein concluded, "If I truly believed in God as the omnipotent author of the historical drama and in Israel as His Chosen People, I had no choice but to accept Dean Gruber's conclusion that Hitler unwittingly acted as God's agent in committing six million Jews to slaughter. I could not believe in such a God, nor could I believe in Israel as the Chosen People of God after Auschwitz" (3).

While Rubenstein's is a stark voice, to some degree he echoes Elie Wiesel's repeated assertion that the only appropriate response to Holocaust is silence. The Holocaust calls memory into question not simply by the effort to destroy the Jewish people entirely, but also because it calls into doubt the memory of a God who delivers.

In Ozick's work, these concerns are most fully seen in a pair of stories in which the command to remember is seen to be the root of ethical behavior. "The Shawl" and "Rosa" focus on a character who, unlike Puttermesser, Bleilip, and others, is all but consumed by the past. Rosa Lublin, like the rebbe of "Bloodshed" and the survivor-guest of "Levitation," is a survivor-victim of the Holocaust who disturbs the present precisely by embodying the past. However, she also represents the Holocaust's rupture because a narrative that links past, present, and future seems all but impossible. In the camps she lost her extended family save for a niece, Stella. She has also lost the future symbolized in her daughter Magda. In "The Shawl" we hear the story of this miraculous child who—concealed in the religiously symbolic wrappings of a shawl—survives for a time in the death camp before being discovered and brutally murdered by a SS guard. Thus, Rosa is metaphorically cut off from both past and future.

"Rosa" asks how Rosa is to live if she cannot articulate a relationship between past and present. Having smashed up her second-hand shop in a rage because customers could not understand her obsession with the Holocaust, Rosa has moved to Florida, where she lives despondently in a community of Jewish retirees. As Rosa says to Persky, the retired button maker who chooses to court her, "Before is a dream. After is a joke. Only during stays. And to call it a life is a lie" (58). Just as she faced an isolated struggle to survive and to protect her child in the death camps, Rosa continues to be isolated in Florida. She lives in a single cramped room in a "hotel" that seems more like a prison cell. But the world outside her solitary confinement proves to be even worse. The Florida "sun was killing" and all too reminiscent of a past life (15); "The streets were a furnace, the sun an executioner" (14). The people living there are all leftovers from the world—detritus, refuse. "Everyone had left behind a real life. Here they had nothing. They were all scarecrows, blown about under the murdering sunball with empty rib cages" (16).

Rosa's incomprehensible past is shown clearly in her relationship to Stella and Persky. These two provide the story with Jewish characters whose modes of relating to the Holocaust differ tremendously from one another and from Rosa's method of recurring constantly to the past. Stella, her niece living in New York, does everything she can to repress the past and "move on" with her life. In a letter to Rosa, Stella tells her that she is sending Rosa the miraculous shawl that had once nurtured Magda. The letter reveals Stella's frustration at Rosa's intransigent attachment to the past. Stella angrily dismisses Rosa's devotion to the shawl: "It's thirty years, forty, who knows, give it a rest" (31).

Stella's mode of dealing with the trauma of the Holocaust is to repress, leaving her unsympathetic to Rosa's obsessive imaginative reconstruction of the death camps.[10] For Stella, whom Rosa calls an "ordinary American," obsession with the past is madness. Rosa's judgment on Stella for her Americanness is summary and unambiguous: "Stella is self-indulgent. She wants to wipe out memory" (58).

While exchanges between Rosa and Stella are virulent, those between Persky and Rosa are more subtle and complicated. A comical seducer, Persky pursues Rosa assiduously. His motives may be self-indulgent since his wife has long lived in an asylum. Nevertheless, he is patient with Rosa's paranoid episodes, and he seems genuinely interested in her. If he admires himself as a flirt, he is compassionate about her losses and understands her erratic ways of dealing with those losses. Moreover, to some degree he seems to represent a form of Jewish memory that has bypassed the Holocaust. Persky immigrated from Poland prior to World War II and keeps up with the Jewish world by reading a Yiddish newspaper.

Yet, this very detour around the Holocaust suggests the difficulty the Holocaust presents for a coherent narrative of Jewish cultural memory. Upon meeting Rosa in a Laundromat and discovering she is from Warsaw, Persky immediately assumes a cultural connection. This marks Persky as "typically American" by assuming the timeless connections of geography outside of history.[11] Rosa, however, is quick to point out the realities of history: "My Warsaw isn't your Warsaw" (19). Persky continues in his conviction of the redemptive power of geography when he begins to sense that Rosa has a troublesome relationship to her past and present as a Jew.

> "In Miami, Florida, people are more friendly. What," he said, "you're still afraid? Nazis we ain't got, even Ku Kluxers we ain't got. What kind of person are you, you're still afraid?"
> "The kind of person," Rosa said, "is what you see. Thirty-nine years ago I was somebody else." (19)

While Persky's belief in the timelessness of geography allows him to insist on connections between all Floridians regardless of history, race, ethnicity, or gender, Rosa invokes the distinctions of historical experience. Thirty-nine years ago she was somebody else. While Persky identifies with all around him because they live in Florida, the Holocaust has left Rosa unable to form a coherent narrative of personal identity.

Characters consumed by the past have been staples of American literature, often created for the express purpose of critiquing the present. In Faulkner's "A Rose for Emily," Emily literally clings to the past represented in her dead lover, asserting the superiority of the past over and against the trivializing forces of the modernizing southern society around her. More recently, in Toni Morrison's *Beloved*, Sethe's murder of her own child and her devotion to the child's ghost primarily reveals the murderousness of the society in which she lives. Similarly, for Ozick, Rosa's obsession highlights the shallow sense of self and community possessed by other characters in the book.

But Rosa is also like Sethe and Emily in that she remains irretrievably isolated by the past which she cannot escape. Emily remains in the house. Sethe lives alone with a child/ghost who gradually becomes vampiric, sucking whatever life remains from Sethe's body. Memory is a destroyer. Similarly, Rosa's embrace of the past does not guard memory. Ozick has suggested that the purpose of memory is for life in the present, to help establish ethical relationships with others in the present (*Metaphor* 279).[12] For Rosa, however, the past is not a resource for responsible relationships with others in the present but a siren song that continually calls her away from responsibility to others. If Stella and Persky's response to the past is shallow and naive, Rosa's is destructive in assuming that she must deny the present and be sucked into the "during." If Stella and Persky make idols of the present moment by freezing it apart from all other moments of the past and future, Rosa makes an idol of the past by believing the present and future cannot matter. All three remove themselves from history and bring an end to cultural memory in different ways. The ironic consequence of this is that the Holocaust will have done its work precisely because it will have created an unbridgeable rupture in the stream of Jewish memory. In the end, Rosa uses the past to separate herself and hold herself aloof from others.

The irony is particularly excruciating because the past Rosa remembers is characterized by assimilation to high Polish culture rather than to any particularly Jewish reality. This is clearest in her fantasized relationship with her dead child, Magda. Just as Puttermesser imagined a child learning Latin, Rosa writes letters to the child she imagines to be "a professor of Greek philosophy" (39). In one letter she reminisces at length about the life destroyed back in Poland—a life, incidentally, marked by class differences and her parents' desire to assimilate: her mother thought about converting to Catholicism and even wrote a poem to the Virgin Mary (41).

In the conclusion of her letter to the imaginary Magda, Rosa writes the following: "Let [Stella] think whatever she thinks; her mind is awry, poor thing; in me the strength of your being consumes my joy. Yellow blossom! Cup of the sun!" (44). Ozick has suggested that idols depend on the devotion and imagination of their devotees for their reality and power.[13] Ironically, however, once that devotion is given, the idol in turn demands sacrifice and consumes the devotee. This structure is clearly at the center of Rosa's relationship with Magda and, analogously, with the whole of her past. The strength of Magda's being "consumes" Rosa. However, Magda's very being— the beautiful and successful professor of philosophy in New York— is generated through Rosa's imagination. Rosa participates in her own destruction. Whatever the limitations of Stella's repression of the past, Stella has seen Rosa's mistake. Stella links Magda's shawl with medieval devotions to false relics: "You're like those people in the Middle Ages who worshiped a piece of the True Cross, a splinter from some old outhouse as far as anybody knew, or else they fell down in front of a single hair supposed to be some saint's. You'll kiss, you'll pee tears down your face, and so what? Rosa, by now, believe me, it's time, you have to have a life" (31–32).

Whatever Stella's limitations, she points out the destructiveness of Rosa's relationship with the past. Rosa's inability to construct a relationship to her present has taken her life. Magda is a bloodsucker.

Thus, Rosa is a more extreme and less humorous inheritor of Puttermesser's problems with isolation. While serving Persky tea in her room, she opens a package that she thinks contains the shawl that she had used in the camps to protect her daughter Magda. When she discovers that the package contains instead a book sent to her by Dr. Tree—a social psychologist interested in doing statistical studies on Holocaust survivors—she flies into an uncontrollable rage, destroys the teacups that she has set out for Persky, and accuses Persky of being a thief. Understandably, Persky hurriedly exits. When the shawl finally does arrive, Rosa holds it as she speaks with Stella over the telephone: "Rosa took the shawl and put it over the knob of the receiver: it was like a little doll's head then. She kissed it, right over Stella's admonitions. 'Good-bye,' she told Stella, and didn't care what it had cost. The whole room was full of Magda. . . . She was wearing one of Rosa's dresses from high school. Rosa was glad: it was the sky-colored dress, a middling blue with black buttons seemingly made of round chips of coal, like the unlit shards of stars. Persky could never have been acquainted with buttons like that, they were so black and so sparkling" (64–65).

While the conversation demonstrates Stella's shortcomings, it also demonstrates Rosa's unethical dismissal of the present. First, the shawl literally smothers the voice of the other. Using the shawl, Rosa turns the telephone into the image of living thing and worships that thing at the expense of a relationship with living human beings. Wrapped in the shawl, the telephone becomes an idol through which Rosa speaks only to herself and things created through her own imagination (Lowin 120). Magda's fantastic appearance in the room and the images that she conjures up for Rosa also cut her off from Persky. Magda's appearance denigrates Persky and his work as a button manufacturer and so helps Rosa maintain a sense of class superiority to others. In this case, memory of the past is not a metaphor by which one comes to live empathetically with others, but one by which Rosa can maintain her superiority to her fellow Jew, Persky. Out of time, Rosa removes herself from possible relationships with other human beings.

After she has ended the phone call with Stella, Rosa begins writing a long letter to Magda in which she tries to explain her life. She recounts the dark time in Poland, especially her stay in the Warsaw ghetto. She recalls seeing common working folk going by on a tramcar through the horror of the ghetto, thinking bitterly that they were now considered superior, despite the high Polish culture her family had acquired. She remembers specifically an old woman carrying home a bag of green lettuce:

> [The] people in the tramcar were regarded as Poles—well, they were, I don't take it away from them, though they took it away from us—and we were not! They, who couldn't read one line of Tuwim, never mind Virgil, and my father who knew nearly the whole first half of the *Aeneid* by heart. And in this place now I am like the woman who held the lettuce in the tramcar. I said all this in my store, talking to the deaf. How I became like the woman with the lettuce. (68–69)

Here the letter breaks off as Rosa is suddenly fatigued. Moreover, to Rosa's astonishment, Magda is slowly turning away, fading. The Jewish Poland that Rosa recalls and treasures is not that of the *shtetl* or of Talmudic learning or even of the simplicity of religious worship. In seeing her similarity to the woman with the lettuce, Rosa implicitly recognizes that she has cut herself off, that she has considered herself superior, that she has tried furiously to forget the Jews. She is a Puttermesser of the Old World.

Rosa, of course, may not realize all this consciously. However, the realization seems to be, at last, a memory that does not pull her helplessly into the past. Immediately upon admitting her identification with the Polish persecution, several events begin to reconnect her to the world. Magda fades away. The telephone begins to ring. The Cuban receptionist announces that Persky is downstairs, waiting to see her. For the first time, Rosa responds not with rejection but with a willingness to see and speak with others. "'He's used to crazy women, so let him come up,' Rosa told the Cuban. She took the shawl off the phone" (70).

Rosa's comment to the receptionist, while ironic, also announces her self-awareness; this is the first moment in the story in which memory draws people together rather than acting as a wall between human relationships. Persky, in fact, has a wife in an institution in New York and through that experience is able to empathize to some degree with Rosa's emotional outbursts. Similarly, Rosa has recognized a malady in herself. What is more important, she has remembered Persky's past, which allows her to identify herself with Persky's deranged wife. While Rosa is self-deprecating, the practice of memory allows Persky and Rosa to come together with some hope for the future. If I am right that Magda is primarily a negative fantasy in the story, then the final lines clearly affirm a life of commerce between past, present, and future. "Magda was not there. Shy, she ran from Persky. Magda was away" (70).

Given the historical context, it is not surprising that Ozick's literature is dominated by cautionary tales, tales that exhort her readers to remember, to never forget. It is also probably not surprising that the substance of cultural memories in Ozick's fiction is relatively fragmentary and sporadic: a legend of a golem in "Puttermesser and Xanthippe," a tale of sacrifice in "Bloodshed," fragmentary and compromised memories of Poland's high Jewish culture in "Rosa." Across a chasm of forgetfulness, one could hardly expect the transmission of cultural memories that reflect "the shared faith, cohesiveness, and will of the [Jewish people]" that Yerushalmi eulogizes (94).

Still, Ozick's work does not, I think, justify Yerushalmi's pessimism when he says that memory cannot be "healed or rejuvenated" (94). Yerushalmi's position depends on two questionable assumptions: that the cohesiveness of memory is unchanging and that the contemporary experience of forgetfulness is unique. In fact, the Jewish tradition of memory is marked not by static transference of timeless religious truth but by liquidity, creativity, and change in response to repeated historical ruptures and lacunae. In the textual traditions of Judaism, the memory I am speaking of has been most often categorized under the broad term *Aggadah*, a primary form of Jewish religious interpretation. As Joseph Heinemann has pointed out, classical *Aggadah* originated in the Palestinian Jewish community as a response to historical threats to the meaning of Jewish life.

> To a certain extent, the *Aggadah* represents a creative reaction to the upheavals suffered by Israel in their land. . . . It also represents an attempt to develop new methods of exegesis designed to yield new understandings

of Scripture for a time of crisis and a period of conflict, with foreign cultural influence pressing from without and sectarian agitation from within. This period demanded a response to the crises brought about by historical events, foremost the destruction of Jerusalem and its Temple and the total loss of political independence. This complex of spiritual, political, and national challenges required constant grappling with problems and taking new stands suited to present needs. (42–43)

Similarly, Jacob Neusner points out that *Genesis Rabbah* and *Leviticus Rabbah*—two compilations of *midrashim* that shaped Judaism in the Common Era—were written in response to the political triumphs of Christianity, triumphs that seemed to belie the notion that God had a special concern for Israel (11). Michael Fishbane suggests that this process by which the past is recuperated for the present is "a generic structure of Jewish tradition" (1).

This discussion indicates that the Jewish relation to tradition has been far more mobile and creative than Yerushalmi's analysis would seem to allow. To be sure, American Judaism in the post-Enlightenment and post-Holocaust period encounters a unique historical problematic. However, that there is a challenge to memory does not mean memory has failed utterly. Rather it means that history again forces Judaism into a creative appropriation of the past, one which recognizes that Judaism itself has always been a hybrid form of historical response and consumption rather than a static set of unchanging doxa. In her various theories of the relationship of the Jewish community to the facts of modernity, Ozick recognizes the importance of this invention of new forms of cultural memory in the face of historical discontinuities. Indeed, she sees the development of Judaism in the Common Era as just such an exemplary invention. The holiness of study in classical Judaism adapts Greek and Platonic modes of thought to a Jewish reality, even though the primordial Jewish texts tell the stories of nomads and shepherds who have little interest in study. By a similar act of cultural appropriation, the new facts of post-Enlightenment history might be redeemed for a tradition of memory, even while recognizing that such memory is not seamless. She says:

> It took generations—a handful of centuries—for the Socratic emphasis on pedagogic exertion to infiltrate the Jewish emphasis on divinely inspired communal responsibility. Undoubtedly it will take another handful of centuries—the two hundred that have elapsed so far are plainly not

enough—for Enlightenment ideas of skepticism, originality, individuality, and the assertiveness of the free imagination to leach into what we might call the Jewish language of restraint, sobriety, moral seriousness, collective conscience. Such a hugely combining project is the work not only of generations, but of giants. It will require fifty Bialiks, each one resplendent with the force of Halachic reverence for the minutiae of conscientiousness. "But where is duty?" Bialik cried into the enchanting face of love and poetry. (Metaphor 237–38)

Ozick's work represents one form of creative response to historical rupture. Her texts are a call to cultural memory and themselves threads of cultural memory, threads that lead readers backward and forward to other threads of tradition. While her work does not by itself heal or rejuvenate Jewish collective memory, it is a mark of that memory and a force that speaks to the possibility of a reimagined Jewish memory for the present.

3

Re-membering the Body in the Work of Alice Walker

Cynthia Ozick's effort to recover Jewish memory emphasizes textual traditions, sometimes to an idiosyncratic extreme that inscribes a stark division between texts and bodies. Indeed, depictions of a specifically Jewish body are all but absent in Ozick's work, as are invocations of the female body as a locus of experiential knowledge. What makes a person Jewish is not a Jewish nose, a Jewish mother, or even endless servings of chicken soup spiced with Yiddishisms. Rather, the Jew must have a Jewish soul, a soul attached to the great historical Jewish ideas that Ozick articulates throughout her work. Similarly, a woman's body does not situate her experience in any particular way, except, perhaps, insofar as she experiences prejudice from others.

The irrelevance of the body to tradition is a theme present throughout Ozick's work, represented, for instance, in "Virility," a story in which a young and hopelessly bad poet steals his aunt's poetry when she dies and publishes it as his own. As a result he is championed as the founder of a new school of virile poetry. When the scam is discovered, the poetry is reassessed as having "a lovely girlish voice" and as being "choked with female inwardness" (*Pagan*

Rabbi 266). While bodies may affect book reviews, Ozick seems to say, they do not affect literature itself. A similar theme preoccupies "The Pagan Rabbi," which opens with the following aphorism: "Rabbi Jacob said: He who is walking along and studying, but then breaks off to remark, 'How lovely is that tree!' or 'How beautiful is that fallow field!'— Scripture regards such a one as having hurt his own being" (3). The story traces the life of Rabbi Kornfeld, an erudite devotee of poetry who falls in love with a wood nymph that embodies the Greek conception of Beauty. Rapturous, Rabbi Kornfeld's body dismisses his rather cranky Jewish soul, a soul who "reads the Law and breathes the dust and doesn't see the flowers and won't heed the cricket spitting in the field" (35). In a final disputation toward the end of the story, soul says to body:

> "If you had not contrived to be rid of me, I would have stayed with you till the end. The dryad, who does not exist, lies. It was not I who clung to her but you, my body. Sir, all that has no real existence lies. In your grave beside you I would have sung you David's songs, I would have moaned Solomon's voice to your last grain of bone. But you expelled me, your ribs exile me from their fate, and I will walk here alone always, in my garden"—he scratched on his page—"with my precious birds"—he scratched at the letters—"and my darling trees"—he scratched at the tall side-column of commentary. . . .
>
> "The sound of the Law," he said, "is more beautiful than the crickets. The smell of the Law is more radiant than the moss. The taste of the Law exceeds clear water." (36)

Faced with the superior truth of the soul and the text, Rabbi Kornfeld's body despairs and ends in suicide.

Ironically, Ozick has partially emphasized this division as a means to overcome the traditional separation of women from the right to study the textual traditions at all. She has compared the monumental loss of Jewish women's contribution to commentary as similar to a Holocaust, and she has disparaged forms of feminism that emphasize the knowledge of the body, seeing such body determinism as fated to play into the hands of patriarchy that has always believed women were all body and no mind or spirit.[1] By emphasizing text as superior to body, Ozick seeks to overcome those who would silence her because she is Jewish and because she is a woman.

But despite Ozick's useful call away from racial and social ephemera to the thickness of a textualized cultural memory, one feels like this emphasis in Ozick is made possible not only by her brilliant mind but also by her white body. As Bonnie TuSmith has pointed out, for nonwhite ethnic groups in a racially polarized United States, race, and therefore the body, are inescapable components of cultural and personal identity (13). While skin color indicates no particular cultural or personal characteristic, the body's racial difference means that the body is an inevitable site of cultural articulation, a field through which community relationships and personal identity are developed and understood.

The body as a site for communal connection is beautifully rendered in the following passage from Toni Morrison, and in it one feels a stark contrast to Ozick's disembodied structures of identity. In this passage, Baby Suggs ministers to the people commanding them to love their bodies, because the body is the site of brokenness.

> "Here," she said, "in this here place, we flesh; flesh that weeps, laughs; flesh that dances on bare feet in grass. Love it. Love it hard. Yonder they do not love your flesh. They despise it. They don't love your eyes; they'd just as soon pick em out. No more do they love the skin on your back. Yonder they flay it. And O my people they do not love your hands. Those they only use, tie, bind, chop off and leave empty. Love your hands! Love them. Raise them up and kiss them. Touch others with them, pat them together, stroke them on your face 'cause they don't love that either. *You* got to love it, *you*! . . . This is flesh I'm talking about here. Flesh that needs to be loved. Feet that need to rest and to dance; backs that need support; shoulders that need arms, strong arms I'm telling you. . . . More than your life holding womb and your life giving private parts, hear me now, love your heart. For this is the prize." Saying no more, she stood up then and danced with her twisted hip the rest of what her heart had to say while the others opened their mouths and gave her the music. Long notes held until the four-part harmony was perfect enough for their deeply loved flesh. (89)

Far from dismissing the body as inferior to the spirit or as unnecessary to community, Baby Suggs sees the body as the necessary route to the spirit and to the persistence of the people. By comparison, Ozick's ethos feels, ironically, somewhat like Stella's repression of the Holocaust. Ozick overcomes the ethnic and female body by denying its significance. By contrast, in *Beloved,* remembering the body con-notes more than a simple recollection of the past. The history of slav-ery is a history of dismemberment. The people over "yonder," beyond the pale of the community in the forest, destroy the black body and have sought to destroy the body of the black community—separating them from home and landscape, separating friend from friend and mother from father and parent from child in the slave auction.

Thus, the domination of African culture in the United States has meant a domination of African cultural memories through the man-agement, dissection, and control of the black body. Baby Suggs's ser-mon calls people to remember the body as something other than what the slave society has forced it to become. She bridges the division between *Eros, Agape,* and *Phileo* common to Western modes of think-ing by insisting that one cannot truly love without loving the body. Becoming a member of the body of the community, reshaping one's own body, and loving bodies of others are all versions of one love.

Alice Walker and the Dis(re)membered Body

In *Beloved,* as in the work of many African American women writ-ers, religious traditions are repositories of memories that help women reshape their bodies and claim them as their own. Remembering one's body opens the self to the world of Spirit through which the stories of one's own life may be reshaped. Among African American women, Alice Walker has been the most persistent investigator of the complicated relationships between memory, the body, spirituality, and community. Moreover, as Ozick has shown that cultural genocide is a complicated combination of communal choices for assimilation and genocidal violence from those outside the community, Walker's work investigates the ways in which the black body is dismembered both through white oppression and through violence perpetrated by the African American community on itself. Often, this violence is upheld by the religious traditions that are otherwise a source of strength. Therefore, her fiction seeks not only to reshape the body in resistance to white domination but also to reshape the traditions of the black community that participate in the community's self-destruction.

These intersections are most evident in Walker's best-known novel, *The Color Purple,* which traces the story of a young and violently abused African American woman, Celie. In the novel, white domination erupts when Sofia, Celie's sister-in-law, is beaten, disfigured, and jailed for refusing to be the white mayor's maid. While working to try to ensure Sofia's release from prison, Mary Agnes, a family friend, is beaten and raped by the town's white sheriff, who also happens to be her cousin. These brutalities are figuratively tied to the larger project of European imperialism through Celie's sister Nettie, who is a missionary in Africa. While in Africa, the traditional ways of the Olinka are broken down when a road built to service the European rubber plantations destroys the village. In each case the bodies of African persons are subject to the interests of white privilege.

However, the given fact of racism is less intriguing than the ways in which African American religion supports domination throughout the story. Celie is a beaten and dominated woman through much of the first half of the story. Moreover, her victimization manifests a cosmic rather than a sociological problem. Celie's God is white and male. Late in the novel, Shug asks Celie to describe God. Celie responds, perhaps predictably, with a description of an old white man with blue eyes. Shug laughs and explains her mirth as follows. When Celie objects to her irreverence, Shug insists that the God of the Bible serves the interests of white people: "How come he look just like them, then? she say. Only bigger? And a heap more hair. How come the bible just like everything else they make, all about them doing one thing and another, and all the colored folks doing is gitting cursed?" (201–2).

At this point late in the novel, Shug can laugh because Celie is already well on the way toward an independent existence. However, early in the novel, the alien character of God merely supports Celie's victimization. If whiteness and maleness signify threats to the bodies of black women, a God who is white and male signifies transcendent violence: all the "colored folks . . . gitting cursed." Celie's worship tends toward passivity and precludes any effective response or resistance to her pain.

Celie's image of God reflects one half of a recognizable dialectic in the history of African American religion in America. On the one hand, religion has served the interests of the master; on the other, it has been transformed and made a source of power for African Americans. Speaking for the moment only of the first half of this dialectic, Hans Baer and Merrill Singer list "five functions that Christianity performed on behalf of slavery":

(1) It provided an ideological rationale for the enslavement of Africans and the social cohesion of white society;

(2) It was part of the deculturation process that the slaves were subjected to after arriving in the Americas;

(3) It had the effect of subduing and pacifying the slaves;

(4) It helped enhance the profitability of the slaves by ensuring their willingness to work hard under adverse conditions.

(5) It functioned to create uniformity among peoples of diverse cultural backgrounds. (4)

To the degree that black Americans accepted the religion of the masters, it served as a powerful form of internalized colonialism.[2] The heavy irony of Celie's religion is not simply that it originates with white people but also that it sustains and is sustained by her family and community. This religion tells her not only how to behave "properly" as a black person but also how to behave "properly" as a woman. An old white male, this God cripples Celie's understanding of herself as an African American and a woman.

As with Baer and Singer's description of slavery, Celie's religion makes her body readily available for degrading work. Celie's life is work. Or, rather, a kind of living death. From the age of fourteen she serves as a human rutting post, expected to service the sexual needs of her stepfather and then husband. Her two children—products of her sexual work and of nine months of "carrying" and of the labor of birth—are stolen from her arms even while she lies in the birthing bed. Her practical position as a slave is symbolized in the horse trading in which Albert and Pa engage to determine her fate.[3] Celie plows Albert's fields, fixes his food, cares for his children, and cleans his house before satisfying his sexual urges in the evening. She even addresses him as a superior, calling him "Mr. ———" through most of the text.

Celie often unconsciously identifies God with the violence she experiences. After she has been raped and impregnated by her stepfather, her mother asks her suspiciously about whose child she is carrying. Celie responds, "God's . . . I don't know no other man or what else to say" (3). The referential ambiguity of "no other man" identifies Celie's stepfather with Celie's God. The only man she knows is her father. Or, rather, the only men she knows are her stepfather and God himself.

This identification is replayed later when Sofia asks Celie why she does not fight Albert's abuse. Celie responds that the Bible has enjoined her to honor her father and mother, and her efforts to follow this injunction have left her stony and emotionless: "Well, sometime Mr. ———— git on me pretty hard. I have to talk to Old Maker. But he my husband. I shrug my shoulders. This life soon be over, I say. Heaven last always. (44)

Celie's justification for her own passivity rests on a fated sense of divine ordination. Her reading of scripture identifies Mr. ————'s interests with God's interests. The last paragraph begins with Mr. ————'s violence. Celie responds with prayer. God's apparent nonanswer, "But he my husband," lets both God and Albert off the hook: being a Christian wife demands submission "no matter what." Furthermore, the ambiguous reference of the pronoun "he" in the paragraph's third sentence refers logically to Mr. ————, but potentially to God: "God is my husband." The story Celie tells in response to the memory of her abuse leads to her futile response: "I shrug my shoulders."

Rosemary Radford Ruether has pointed out that under patriarchy, women and children can only be related to a masculine God through the mediating presence of the male—whether the male priest or the divine son—which thus ensures the woman's passive obedience to the male who is apparently made more in the image of God than she is herself (53–54). Similarly, Celie's understanding of God engenders a resigned act of devotion written in the prayer letters that make up the text. Many critics have made much of the strength of Celie's voice. However, few critics note that her voice champions a spirituality that encourages passivity; Celie observes her life magnificently without doing anything to change it.[4] Her life on earth is to be endured in deference to a meaningful life hereafter.

The Personal Politics of Conversion

According to Walker's construction, then, the Christian God removes himself from the world, as do those who worship him. Life in the body does not count. To some degree this construction reflects a simple fact of life for many women in many Christian churches. Although African American churches have been relatively more open to female leadership than white Protestant and Roman Catholic churches, basic structures have remained largely patriarchal. Black women have had to defer to the prerogatives of male leadership, often figured in the person of the preacher or other church leaders. This expectation found its various incarnations in the movements for Civil Rights and Black Power. For instance, the Southern Christian Leadership Conference resisted the leadership of Ella Baker (Branch 231–32). Infamously, Stokely Carmichael of the Student Nonviolent Coordinating Committee suggested that the only position for women in the movement was "prone" (Wallace 7). The Nation of Islam implicitly suggested that women were little more than chattel (Giddings 317). Until the early 1980s, black theology had relatively little to say about the liberation of black women (Grant 141–46). Indeed, Walker's work has been one of the prime catalysts forcing theologians to account for the experiences of women of color.

Walker's critique of Christianity resonates with other African American critiques. Indeed, African American artists and intellectuals have consistently agonized over the cultural and political role of the church. Frederick Douglass rejected the Christianity he received from slaveholders in favor of the "Christianity of Christ" that he associated with the abolitionist movement. More pointedly, Du Bois accused black churches of complicity in the era of slavery and of ethical irresponsibility during the period following Reconstruction: "[The Negro] churches are differentiating,—now into groups of cold, fashionable devotees, in no way distinguishable from similar white groups save in color of skin; now into large social and business institutions catering to the desire for information and amusement of their members, warily avoiding unpleasant questions both within and without the black world, and preaching in effect if not in word: *Dum vivimus, vivamus*" (504–5).

Picking up the tone of this peroration in the 1930s, Langston Hughes dismissed the Christian God as weak and ineffectual in his well-known poem, "Goodbye Christ." This kind of criticism crested during the Black Power movement of the sixties and seventies, when Alice Walker came of age as a writer. Malcolm X derided Christianity as a religion of the oppressor and encouraged conversion to the Nation of Islam. In *Soul on Ice,* Eldridge Cleaver associates King's nonviolence with James Baldwin's homosexuality, seeing both as degrading and suicidal.[5] In one of the most extreme examples of the criticism of Christianity, Jimmy Garrett concludes his play "We Own the Night" by having his revolutionary protagonist shoot his hypocritical and white-loving Christian mother while proclaiming, "We're . . . new men, Mama . . . Not niggers. Black men" (540).

As with many other revolutionary American rhetorics, such a rhetoric of conversion burns its bridges to the "sinful" past, making such a bridge undesirable at worst and haphazard at best. To some degree this structure of conversion poses the same dilemmas for the continuity of African American culture as were posed in Ozick by the problem of assimilation. If becoming a New Black Man or Woman entails putting off the Old Negro, then how may African Americans articulate a coherent narrative of relationship to the cultural past that does not result in a simple erasure. At the extreme, as evidenced in Garrett's play, it does not, and the black revolutionary shoots his Christian mother.

Alice Walker works in the space of this tension between Newness and Oldness. On the one hand, she has been a clear and consistent critic of Christianity and has participated in the general call for some kind of spiritual/cultural conversion. In her novels, characters who are in touch with an earth-centered spirituality are repositories of vast and ancient wisdom that provides for a renewed and more positive existence. On the other hand she has resisted the cultural amputation that can accompany conversion narratives. For instance, she has insisted on the spiritual strength and vitality of the black Christian church. At one point she remarks that the African American woman's greatest act of creation in the New World has been the transformation of Christianity into a religion of liberation (*Gardens* 17–18). In her early poetry she struggles with the black arts' rhetoric of revolution precisely because it dismisses one's immediate elders. She insists on the importance of remembering earlier generations:

> To acknowledge our ancestors means
> we are aware that we did not make
> ourselves, that the line stretches
> all the way back, perhaps, to God; or
> to Gods. We remember them because it
> is an easy thing to forget: that we
> are not the first to suffer, rebel,
> fight, love and die. . . . (*Petunias* 1)

Similarly, in the poem "In These Dissenting Times," she insists on the value of those black Americans who did not share everything of black arts ideology.

> I shall write of the old men I knew
> And the young men
> I loved
> And of the gold toothed women
> Mighty of arm
> Who dragged us all
> To church. (*Petunias* 2)

Thus Walker's work evinces both halves of the dialectic that I discussed earlier. On the one hand, Christianity has been a source of oppression. On the other hand, Christianity has been a source of strength. Her work embodies the tension between a revolutionary rhetoric that transcends the past by dismissing it and a transformative rhetoric that maintains connection to the past by reimagining it. This tension between connection to the past and the need for revolutionary change animates much of *The Color Purple*. Celie is clearly a character in need of conversion away from stories that have subdued her body. However, how may this be accomplished without losing the community which has been shaped by such stories?

There is no simple answer to that question. In seeking an answer, Walker inscribes a process of remembering with others. A community of women helps Celie remember her body and remember her broken past in a way that is empowering. At the same time, this process of remembering enables Celie to enter into more mutually productive relationships with others.

Ironically, in one way or another almost all the women of the text help Celie change her life except Celie's own mother. Because her mother lives entirely within the domestic range of Celie's stepfather's abuse, she seems finally unable to offer Celie anything but her suspicions, resentment, and pain. Celie's new life as a woman must be "mothered" by a variety of women throughout the text. Her sisters-in-law encourage her to resist their brother Albert. When Celie tells Sofia that she accepts Albert's beatings because she is waiting for heaven, Sofia encourages her to return Albert blow for blow and "think bout heaven later" (44). Even a minor and fairly passive character such as Mary Agnes seems to provide a useful model for Celie as she chooses to change her life and become a singer. In each case these women demonstrate their independence from the men around them, as well as a willingness to change and do something new with their lives when it becomes necessary.

The most important women in Celie's transformation are her sister Nettie and the blues singer Shug Avery. Many readings of the novel privilege Shug and her role in Celie's sexual awakening, seeing it as superior to Nettie's rather formal and distant letters, which seem more like dry echoes of the past. While it is clear that the two women play different roles, their purposes are complementary rather than contrasting. Shug Avery's love opens Celie to her own worth and to the erotic pleasures available through her body. The pleasure she brings Celie through sexual arousal and romantic love reshapes Celie's body and puts the lie to the memories of her body's enslavement. Similarly, through her letters, Nettie reconfigures Celie's memories, enabling her to open out toward the future in a way that even Shug's eroticism cannot.

Celie's memories of her own body primarily include pain and self-alienation. Because her memories of sex are of violation, she thinks of her body as designed to provide pleasure for others rather than personal pleasure or self-expression. Shug Avery helps her imagine her body differently. When Celie first sees Shug's picture, the photograph attracts her erotic attention, and when Shug first arrives at Albert's house, Celie feels sexually aroused. Shug first discovers the extent of Celie's self-alienation as they discuss the fact of Shug sleeping with Celie's husband, Albert. Shug is astounded that Celie seems never to have experienced sexual pleasure at all.

> Naw, I say. Mr. ——— can tell you, I don't like it at all. What is it like? He git up on you, heist your nightgown round your waist, plunge in. Most times I pretend I ain't there. He never know the difference. Never ast me how I feel, nothing. Just do his business, get off, go to sleep.
>
> She start to laugh. Do his business, she say. Do his business. Why, Miss Celie. You make it sound like he going to the toilet on you. (81)

Celie's alienation is so extreme that Shug proclaims her "a virgin" and begins introducing her to an erotic life, teaching her to masturbate (81). Like her literary cousin, Baby Suggs in *Beloved*, Shug emphasizes the transforming power of touching oneself and others, breaking down the walls between eros and other forms of human attachment. Celie and Shug become lovers, and through Shug's love Celie comes gradually to love herself. Self-love and the love of others are symbiotic.

The connection between erotic experience and individual self-realization is enlarged by connection to Shug's spirituality, which reconfigures God as a being who desires human pleasure of every sort. But before that spirituality can be achieved, Celie has first to reconnect with her sister Nettie, from whom she has been separated by Albert's brutality and deception. In need of a personal conversion, Celie is rooted up from her personal history, oddly enough, by Nettie's letters. I say "oddly enough" since Nettie is an exemplar of a black middle-class Christianity that Celie—and Walker—eventually rejects. Indeed, most critics have been disappointed with the tone of Nettie's letters. TuSmith goes so far as to suggest that Nettie's language indicates that she has "lost something—her connectedness to black folk culture and the spirit of the people" (80). This loss is especially pronounced when compared to the connected and communitarian qualities of Celie's folk idiom. Nor does Nettie display the freewheeling and rebellious qualities of Shug Avery, who seems somehow more in touch with the values of contemporary feminism.

Nevertheless, I see much more in Nettie than such criticisms have allowed. Even after becoming Shug's lover, Celie remains with Albert, accepts occasional beatings from him, and displays little consciousness that this is an unnatural situation (115). Celie's lassitude reflects her earlier passivity. While some critics have tended to read *The Color Purple* as a lesbian romance in which Shug rescues Celie, such readings miss the ways in which Celie remains in need of change even after her relationship with Shug is firmly established. She remains in need of a larger community of women and especially in need of stories and memories of her own possibility.

Such stories come from Nettie's supposedly formal and "non-oral" voice. Indeed, it is worth remembering that Nettie's "educated" voice is one of Walker's voices—the graduate of Sarah Lawrence—and also the voice of most of Walker's novels, such as *Meridian*, *Temple of My Familiar*, and *Possessing the Secret of Joy*. Moreover, Nettie's voice is a voice achieved partially because she has been able to exercise freedoms of which Celie could only dream. Nettie was allowed to go to school while Celie was forced to stay home and service her father's sexual and domestic needs. I appreciate TuSmith's emphasis on the communitarian values of Celie's voice, but it must also be recognized that the miniature community of her homespace has been the primary site of her oppression. By contrast, Nettie's voice indicates the possibility of a different trajectory and a different life. In short, Nettie is like Celie, but with different memories and different possibilities for her future.

Thus, Nettie's letters provide Celie with new stories and new images of a possible life. She shares Celie's origins and her experience of spiritual marginalization. Like Celie, she faces sexism, in her case through the everyday practices of the Olinka tribe to which she ministers, practices so naturalized that the women work even more than the men to reinforce traditional roles and taboos. Nettie explicitly links these practices to her own biography, saying that the Olinka men treated the women much as "Pa" had treated Celie and Nettie in America (168).

However, Nettie also provides a counterpoint to Celie's complacency.[6] Unlike Celie, Nettie has challenged the sexist practices around her, and through Christianity she has developed a work for herself that is empowering and self-affirming. She has even questioned those aspects of her own faith that seem inadequate to her experience. Within a received Christianity that she is willing to alter to empower herself and others, she finds work not totally subsumed to male desire. Within the ideals of Christian love she develops a relationship with a man, Samuel, not characterized by domination and abuse. Thus, even given the bleak picture that *The Color Purple* elsewhere paints of Christianity, it is Nettie, the Christian missionary, who imagines and lives a creative life at least partially free from patriarchal domination. Nettie appropriates and molds the Christian rhetoric of the transcendent justice of God, a rhetoric that African American Christians have found vital to their experience in America, to move beyond the strictures of traditional female roles.[7] In modeling this life for Celie, Nettie points to the possibility of life outside and away from Albert and the roles he has forced Celie to fulfill.

Nettie not only embodies a different history, she creates a new history for Celie, thus providing for a new consciousness that is a precondition for change. Until Celie discovers the letters from Nettie that Albert has hidden, Celie has imagined herself as a victim of incest, her sibling/children dead in the forest somewhere at the hand of her/their father. Nettie's letters begin to create a new imagination and a new material presence. When she first begins reading Nettie's letters, Celie says, "Now I know Nettie alive, I begin to strut a little bit. Think, When she come home us leave here. Her and me and our two children" (154).

Moreover, one of Nettie's letters shatters the story of Celie's origins with the revelation "Pa is not our Pa!" (182), as if to say, "We are not who we thought we were." By re-creating Pa as stepfather rather than father, Nettie clears a space in which Celie can bring new imaginative possibilities to life. Celie is figuratively reborn. Upon learning that she is not Pa's progeny, she begins to make plans with Shug to leave Albert. Celie no longer merely records the story others have told for her but begins to imagine a future story written by and for herself in which she participates in a family and community she has never been allowed to have. In revealing that "Pa is not our Pa," Nettie has revealed more than a genetic fact about Celie's body. Given the identification of divine authority, patriarchy and racism— an identification that has determined Celie's oppression—to say that "Pa is not our Pa" undermines and cracks the foundations of an oppressive form of life. To say "Pa is not our Pa" is to say that the stories that a racist and patriarchal imagination have told Celie are simply lies. With lies revealed, new possibilities for living may emerge.

Among those new possibilities are the possibilities of a different orientation to the world at large. With the falsehood of male stories exposed, Celie is freed to begin imagining God differently. The immediate source of these new possibilities is Shug Avery. Shug's spirituality constructs a world for Celie that provides for creativity and life rather than death. This spirituality emphasizes creation and celebration in an effort to transform the world, particularly the world of work in which Celie has found herself oppressed. Shug therefore draws on a strong tradition of praise and celebration associated with African American religions. The importance of celebration for African American religions can be traced to a sustained African heritage. It is also expressed in Christian imperatives to celebrate in the midst of evil (Wilmore 12–13). While such celebration in the presence of evil is not in and of itself sufficient for a completely changed life, it functions in ways similar to Bahktin's notion of the carnival: celebration, laughter, and joy are a kind of excess or surplus which point beyond the meaning assigned to black existence by racist ideologies and practices.[8] Celebration mocks the racist and sexist designation of black womanhood as the nadir of human existence. Celebration joyfully affirms the difference of blackness, a joy that exceeds and reconfigures life's serious enterprise.

Since God as white and male undergirds Celie's life as a slave, valuable only insofar as she is productive sexually and economically, Shug's spirituality reinterprets God by identifying divinity with a holy pleasure. Shug's God is a God who glories in a ubiquitous pleasure, pleasure perceivable even in the midst of what Celie has heretofore only known as work: the color purple in a field, sex, sewing, relationships with children, and even relationships with men. Shug describes God as "everything" (202). Shug's spirituality makes God, into a more personal, a more intimate God, so intimate that Celie may feel this Spirit charging along the very lines of her own flesh and bone. This makes radical the personal and practical character of God in many black religions. This omnipresence is not passive, for what good could a God be who is there but can do nothing? Rather, God is also omnipotent, the divine potency being revealed not as an abstract possibility, but in the fact of God's creative agency, God everywhere infusing everything with an explosive creative potential.

Reflecting African American combinations of Western and African traditions, this divine creativity resonates both with Christian identifications of God as the good creator and sustainer, and with Yoruba understandings of Ashe, the divine potentiality upon which human beings may draw in their own enterprise (Thompson 3–10). This emphasis on creativity is so fundamental that God's wrath expresses itself not in destruction but in creative acts. When God is angered, Shug assures Celie, It creates to bring people pleasure (203).[9] In this narrative, God's activity transforms the world, making it the locus of creativity rather than a static and timeless oppression. Here, God is primarily Creator. Moreover, "It" creates for human pleasure, desiring human pleasure as a proper response. Worship manifests itself as pleasure, what Shug calls "admiration" or what I have been calling celebration.

This picture of a God who desires joy stands in stark contrast to the God before whom Celie has stood guilty and ashamed. Celebration demands that the oppressed and those committed to their liberation use creativity to change the historical situation in which they find themselves imprisoned.[10] Implicit within a discourse

55

that celebrates the creation and the Creator as good is the possibility of a liberating practice that imitates the Creator in work. Just as God created the world and called it good, just as the world continues to create and re-create itself in the process of death and regeneration, Celie too may re-create her own life to reflect and partake of the general fecund nature of the creation itself. Creation is one metaphor for unalienated labor, a model and a utopian hope for those who are alienated from their own lives. The celebration of creation entails the demand that one create in imitation of the object of celebration. In this sense, God, reborn in the womb of Shug's spirituality, becomes Celie's ultimate model, the new stories about "It" her ultimate gospel.

Work, Religion, and Domesticity

Critics often emphasize the novel's development up to Celie's escape from Albert, treating the novel in the classic terms of the conversion narrative. Progress is made from darkness into the light that is occasioned by receiving the gospel or, in this case, Nettie's letters. The novel itself seems to break when Celie leaves behind her husband and her old God for her new lover and her lover's creative spirit. As Celie says at her point of departure, "I'm pore, I'm black, I may be ugly and can't cook, a voice say to everything listening. But I'm here. Amen, say Shug. Amen, amen" (214). This has the feel of a dramatic declaration of independence that could well have brought the novel to a close. However, the novel does not end, continuing on for a full quarter of its length from the apparent point of Celie's conversion to a better way of life.

While the story may continue for many reasons, the uncertain relationship between Celie's newfound spirituality and her everyday life is crucial. Celie must both continue the process of shaking off her old self, and find ways that the new self can even begin to live. As Shug says to Celie, "You have to git man off your eyeball, before you can see anything at all" (204). To which Celie responds, "But this hard work, let me tell you. He been there so long, he don't want to budge" (204). While Celie's oppression has been enabled by her false memories and her false religion, changing those elements of her life does not happen automatically nor does it automatically free her from the life she has been living. Given that life with Albert is almost the only life she has known, what kind of life will enable her to "git man off [her] eyeball"? Indeed, Celie faces the knotty problem of how to make a life at all, to say nothing of figuring out how her spirituality is related to that life. In untangling that issue, Celie bounces up against many of the traditional problems, and opportunities, that are afforded by the idealization of domestic arrangements in American religious history.

In reflecting on the various ways in which African American women have contributed to the struggle for civil rights in America, bell hooks suggests that historically

> African-Americans have recognized the subversive value of homeplace, of having access to private space where we do not directly encounter white racist aggression. Whatever the shape and direction of black liberation struggle (civil rights reform or black power movement), domestic space has been a crucial site for organizing, for forming political solidarity. Homeplace has been a site of resistance. Its structure was defined less by whether or not black women and men were conforming to sexist behavior norms and more by our struggle to uplift ourselves as a people, our struggle to resist racist domination and oppression. (Yearning 47)

I would probably extend hooks's point here to a variety of other ethnic groups as well. The home as the repository of language, storytelling, religion, cultural festivals, and memories is seen by many ethnic groups as the particular site of cultural empowerment over and against the aggressive homogenizing tendencies of the public sphere.

What intrigues me in hooks's narrative is the degree to which it conforms to the public/private divisions that have structured American society since the nineteenth century, both in terms of ethnicity and gender. As I already suggested in my discussion of Cynthia Ozick, one classic configuration of ethnicity in America has endorsed ethnicity at home as long as ethnic differences disappear in the street for the sake of the public good. Thus the home becomes a resource for ethnic power because it is the space in which it is allowed freely to appear. This division is also traditionally evident in American gendered relationships. As early as Harriet Beecher Stowe, women writers recognized domestic space as a source of political opposition. In her novel *Uncle Tom's Cabin*, Stowe opposes the communitarian values of the domestic sphere to the public brutalities of the fugitive slave law. This is made clear in an exchange between Senator and Mrs. Bird as to what an appropriate Christian response to a fugitive slave should be.

> "But, Mary, just listen to me. Your feelings are all quite right, dear, and interesting, and I love you for them; but, then, dear, we mustn't suffer our feelings to run away with our judgment; you must consider it's not a matter of private feeling,—there are great public interests involved,—there is such a state of public agitation rising, that we must put aside our private feelings."
>
> "Now, John, I don't know anything about politics, but I can read my Bible; and there I see that I must feed the hungry, clothe the naked, and comfort the desolate; and that Bible I mean to follow."
>
> "But in cases where your doing so would involve a great public evil—"
>
> "Obeying God never brings on public evils. I know it can't. It's always safest, all around, to *do as He* bids us." (100–101)

Mrs. Bird demonstrates the irony of an apparently world-informing faith that can speak only in the restricted several square feet of home and hearth. Mrs. Bird does not agitate in the marketplace for her religious ideals but remains content to agitate with her husband at the hearth.

Thus, homespace is an ambivalent space in American religious and political history: on the one hand, it offers an alternative to the "male" and "white" values of the public sphere; on the other hand, insofar as it is clearly domestic, its relationship to public life remains contained and muzzled. Much like theology in the story of Walter Benjamin's puppet, homespace is a complicated space of empowerment and containment.

In Walker's work homespace seems to be as much a problem as a resource. Walker's novels are populated by women for whom home and tradition are ambivalent sites of oppression as much as empowerment. In *Temple of My Familiar,* Walker revisits the characters of *The Color Purple,* creating a daughter for Olivia named Fanny. The primary block to Fanny's development as a woman is not racism, though there is that, but the desiccated emotional life she leads at home with her husband, who is a professor of American history. In *By the Light of My Father's Smile,* a character named June leads a self-destructive life at least in part because she was brutally beaten by her father when she became sexually active. While Walker suggests that June's father abused her because of a fanatic desire to embody the principles of white, middle-class Protestantism, she also recognizes such "domestic" violence need not be linked to racism. Indeed, even in *The Color Purple,* Nettie makes a point of telling Celie that the men of the Olinka tribe treat the women as the white people treat black people in America. Here racism is an analogue, not a cause.

Such domestic violence can also be inflicted by women on one another. In *Possessing the Secret of Joy,* she revisits the characters of *The Color Purple.* Tashi, the African wife of Celie's son Adam, struggles to overcome the psychological effects of the genital mutilation inflicted on her by an African woman. She is devastated by memories of her mother's complicity in her sister's mutilation, a bloody affair that ended in the sister's painful death. Homespace, in Walker's work, need not be safe space.

Viewed in this light, Walker's close link between sexual self-discovery and spirituality underscores the difficult relationship between private and public space. Walker seems most confident in imagining the human transformations that are possible in face-to-face relationships, relationships that are at their most intense at the heights of sexual ecstasy. But how that ecstatic moment, removed from the censuring eye of church or husband or law, can be translated to a larger social arena remains difficult and problematic. The religion she receives from Shug is the religion of a very public, nearly antidomestic woman: a blues singer who travels the country with multiple lovers, having given up her children to be raised by relatives. But this religion does not translate easily to Celie's situation.

Initially, Celie finds a temporary niche within a communal economy, leaving Albert and the Georgia countryside for Shug and Memphis. She moves beyond passive admiration for the creative acts of God and into an imitative agency in which she herself becomes creator with a small *c*, the author of her own history. This creative potential is expressed in Celie's pants-making, a form of jazz improvisation that, in its own way, replicates Shug's singing. Celie designs her pants to fit the specific needs of those in her immediate community: Odessa, Shug, Shug's band members, Squeak, Jack. Moreover, Celie's livelihood does not depend on her ability to produce the pants: the pants themselves have not yet become market commodities. Rather Shug provides for her according to her needs, asking each week, "How much money you think you need this week?" (219).

This statement suggests a degree of ambiguity in this newly developing family without relatives. The luminous possibility of a new community glimmers fleetingly, a community in which each member provides for others according to his or her own special talents or interests. However, in providing the money necessary for living, Shug replicates many of the traditional arrangements of marital life. Being freed from Albert's beatings is indeed freedom for Celie, as is the freedom to do productive work that she seems to enjoy, especially when compared to the horror or work for her stepfather and for Albert. However, Shug's statement also suggests that Celie continues to live within an economy of dependence. Even Celie seems to recognize this as she first tells Shug that she needs to give up what she's doing and find a job. While Shug short circuits this suggestion by setting up Celie in a pants-making cottage industry, the final quarter of the novel faces the ambiguity of Celie's independence rather than celebrating her deliverance from oppression.

Once Celie's small business is operating, Celie's sewing drops almost completely from view, as does every mention of spirituality. Indeed, she apparently no longer sews or prays at all, but only designs, leaving the sewing to other women, Jerene and Darlene, who enjoy it. This new situation also seems to drain the joy from Celie's life. As soon as Celie is independent, Shug leaves Celie for a man. Celie is left without even her love of sewing. After getting the business up and running, Celie only speaks of it in one context, mentioning that she is making pants for pregnant women, and even the thought of someone pregnant saddens her (224). The early specificity of her enterprise, in which each pair of pants expresses love for and fills the needs of a specific loved person, is abstracted to fit the generic needs of a generic category, "pregnant women." The mass production of the pants has clearly empowered Celie, but at a difficult price. The pants have become commodities and the wearers have become faceless consumers. Economic independence seems to have provided Celie with an identity apart from male domination, apart from Albert, apart from God, even apart from Shug. But this also suggests that it has abstracted her from the communities that made her work pleasant and meaningful to begin with.

Walker's solution to this difficulty is ambiguous, but also, I think, more complicated than she has sometimes been given credit for. It is clear, for instance, that the fundamental solution depends heavily on a return to the domestic scene. Fortuitously provided a home and inheritance on the occasion of her stepfather's death, Celie returns to Georgia, where she reconfigures her relationship with Albert, renews her relationship with Shug, and reestablishes herself as a mother upon her children's homecoming. These last pages collect Celie's history into the domestic frame of her house, suggesting that it is within that frame that she will attempt to reconcile the conflicts and agonies of history.

The utopian and sentimental elements of this conclusion have bothered a number of critics. Indeed, it is clear that Walker is given, in most of her novels, to what could be described as a sentimental push for resolution. Compared to the haunting, ambiguous, and even terrifying conclusion of Morrison's *Beloved*—where we are told that this "was not a story to pass on" (275)—Walker's conclusions seem to come tied with a bow. In *Possessing the Secret of Joy,* Tashi is executed for killing the woman who performed her genital mutilation, but as she dies she is looking at a sign being held by her loved ones, saying, "RESISTANCE IS THE SECRET OF JOY," and we hear her voice from the grave proclaiming that she is satisfied (279). In *By the Light of My Father's Smile,* the reader is privy to the conversations of father and abused daughter after death, conversations in which daughter forgives father and both are reconciled.

This having been said, it seems important to at least grant Walker's premise of a move beyond simple realism and examine the function of the sentimentality and utopianism within her novels. Most important, the sentimentalism in *The Color Purple* does not move simplistically. A tradition of sentimental romance, for instance, is to simply erase history and the specificity of memories. Separated daughters and mothers are reunited on the final pages of such novels. Apparently dead children are not really dead at all. An apparently ugly ducking merely needs a lover to turn into a swan. Pa is not our Pa. Obviously all of these elements are present in Walker's novel, but the final scene also suggests that Walker is working with and against these motifs.

Rather than simply replace the evil domesticity with a good domesticity at the end, there is a more comprehensive effort to reimagine what a healthy domestic community might mean at all. This new imagination emphasizes the significance of shared memories of mutuality rather than assigning some form of natural meaning to biological roles. For instance, while Celie is reunited with her children, there is no simplistic reassertion of the biological imperatives of motherhood. Indeed, Celie comments on how handsome and beautiful her children are, but also on how there is a degree of distance between the generations. Similarly, while she is reunited with Nettie, there is no assertion of the priority of biological relationship. Given her history, Celie understands Shug and Albert as "her people," as the people of her home, the people who share her memories.

The community present at the end of the novel seems less a community built on biological relationship and social obligation than one built on mutual respect and love. The persons in the community are from diverse cultural and familial backgrounds—African, African American, animist, Christian, male, female, gay, straight; in short, a hybrid community appropriate to the diverse histories and peoples that constitute it, a community that respects their multiple histories and differences. While she is mother, while she is lover, Celie is able to be and do things apart from the repressive institutions of domesticity. Homespace here has been valorized, not because homespace is inevitably important to ethnic groups but because these people have been transformed by their common struggles, memories, and stories.

Given the centrality of memory to this process of transformation in Celie's life, it is appropriate that the novel concludes with an evocation of cultural memory on the Fourth of July. Since this novel concerns deliverance from a form of slavery, I have often imagined that it would have been appropriate to have the novel end on Juneteenth, the African American celebration of release from slavery. But having the novel conclude on the Fourth of July calls up the necessity of living within a culture filled with oppressive memories but learning to live those memories differently. On the Fourth of July the family gathers to celebrate "each other," as Harpo puts it, because, "White people busy celebrating they independence from England July 4th, say Harpo, so most black folks don't have to work" (294).

The possibility for celebration, for symbolizing utopia, comes at a time when "black folks don't have to work," when, in other words, the everyday systems of the world arrest themselves. Of course, on the one hand, the Fourth of July merely represents another holy day affirming the values of American culture, the mythology of freedom and opportunity that the oppression in the book belies on every hand. The stories told on the Fourth of July are those of the "founding fathers," the Great Men whose memory seeks to trivialize stories of black women from the Deep South. However, this Sabbath is reinterpreted by the folks of Celie's community in a way that offers the possibility of celebrating their own values and dignity. America, here, is remembered, but remembered differently. This memory and celebration reflects the spirituality that Shug introduced to Celie in the initial moments of her transformation. Now the implications of that spirituality point beyond a simple assertion of Celie's independence and suggest the possibility of community and connection.

The religion of the home at the end of *The Color Purple* is thus domestic religion with a difference precisely because it allows for a homespace not characterized by domination as homespaces all too often are. The home at the end of the novel no longer perpetuates Celie's domination but rather provides a space from which alternatives to prevailing cultural systems can be imagined.

This imagining is clearest in the final chapter, when Celie returns at last to prayer. Having gotten man off her eyeball, she prays to Shug's God, who is characterized by the beauty that is in every created thing. Significantly, this newfound faith not only provides Celie with hope but also alters her conception of herself in relationship to others. Earlier in the book, when she has lost faith in the God of her fathers and has only just begun the struggle to believe in Shug's God, Celie's new character is apparently brought to a symbolic fulfillment when she describes her success as a businesswoman (Pryse 17). For the first time in the novel, Celie signs her name to a letter, symbolically announcing this work as a product of her own life in the same manner that the pants are her own products as well. All but two of the subsequent letters bear the mark of that individuality in her signed name at the close; by her signature she asserts herself as "Celie," author of her own words and life. However, the final letter, and the novel itself, closes simply with "Amen," marking Celie not as writer or producer, but as one who prays.

The absence of Celie's name suggests that the novel is more than a narrative of Celie's journey toward personal identity, as if Celie were merely another in a long line of individualists common to American romance. The novel suggests instead that personal identity is only found in human relationship and in a harmonious relationship to the cosmic order that the final letter invokes.

In *The Color Purple* this human community is a sign of hope, found, somewhat like the saying of prayers or the reading of novels, in the spaces where the busy processes of everyday life cease. This hope is underscored in the novel's final "Amen." Popularly, the word *Amen* may simply signify closure; however, the novel's final "Amen" reveals the nature of prayer as hope, hope for that which is not yet realized and is articulated only in a stumbling manner. This final "Amen" suggests the meaning of original Greek and Hebrew from which it is derived—"Let it be so." This eschatological vision suggests that what Celie can see now only as a glimmer on the surface of the moving waters of history—a community of love and support and admiration—is what must be made real in the world, fashioned into a fit temple for humanity and for God.

4

Memory, Place, and Ritual in Silko's Ceremony and Almanac of the Dead

When Alice Walker imagines the Fourth of July at the end of *The Color Purple,* she evokes the great narrative of national remembrance in the United States. It is an act of nation-founding that, as Benedict Anderson suggests, requires a necessary remembering and forgetting in order to establish the imagined community of the nation (204–6). On the one hand, the Fourth of July is a story of those who have come before, connecting our current way of life with those who preceded us. On the other hand, the Fourth of July is Independence Day, a memory of rupture that insists upon America's difference from the national, cultural, and religious stories that preceded the stories of the United States. More, this memory of freedom requires the "forgetting" of all those upon whose unwilling sacrifice the national freedom depends, such as the African slaves or the dispossessed of the Native American tribes.

The Color Purple speaks to these ambiguities. The freedom which the Fourth of July memorializes must be remembered differently by those excluded from the national narratives. Thus, Africans and African Americans create a community at odds with the most narrow tales of American liberty, without pretending to dismiss those stories as would the most extreme forms of Afrocentric theorizing. We might say that the community of the home at the end of *The Color Purple* is a community to the side of the dominant national narrative, a community on the margin that translates and transforms the national narratives without abandoning them altogether. Thus while Walker embraces a unique version of domestic American religion, with all the communitarian impulses it inscribes, she is unwilling to abandon the stories that modernity has made available to black women. While remembering the body allows Walker to counter the narratives that dismember the black woman's body and the black community, identity located in the body allows her to maintain the narrative of individual expression and fulfillment so common to the American story.

Thus both "home" and "America" become hybrid spaces in her work, spaces that enable provisional forms of freedom for the women she imagines. Her critique of the United States as a political entity is unmistakable. Yet she often locates the values of individual freedom and expressiveness within the idea or symbol of American liberty. Similarly, "home" is a space of symbolic self-fulfillment, but these homes are constructed in ways that free them from the compulsory allegiances of biological relationships. As Trudier Harris has pointed out in a critique of community in black women's literature, many of these literary communities are collections of female peers who bypass traditional communities established through family lines, male/female interrelationships, and across generational divides (see Harris, "From Exile"). In so doing these literary women create their homes where they find them, and they re-create standard notions of "America" in the process. Freedom that is afforded by spiritual renewal is not connected to a specific time or people but by the changed consciousness and embodied experience of loving individuals creating and maintaining community.

This tendency to deemphasize places and people inherited through biological relationships differentiates the uses of religion in the work of Alice Walker and Leslie Silko. Paula Gunn Allen has said that the most succinct and useful definition of Native American identity is "We are the land" ("Landscape" 7). Or, as Silko herself puts it, "The people and the land are inseparable" (*Yellow Woman* 85). For many Native American tribes, as for the Pueblo of Leslie Silko's heritage, "being the land" means belonging to a specific place and a specific people who endure through centuries if not millennia. According to one theorist, for a people like the Laguna Pueblo, "land is not something one controls as a consequence of individual action, but something with which one shares a particular relationship by virtue of membership in a particular community" (Cornell 39). Every mountain is to be respected, but not every mountain is *Kawaishtyima,* the mountain on Laguna Pueblo that is believed to be the site of the *shipap,* the place of the Pueblo emergence from an underground third world to the fourth world of their contemporary existence. Being "earth-centered," as is Alice Walker, and believing that *Kawaishtyima* is the center of the earth are related but two clearly distinct realities.

This makes the relationship to religion and community difficult for Silko in ways that it is not for Walker. "Remembering the earth" is complicated in that the specific landscape upon which the people depend has been forgotten or destroyed. For instance, *Kawaishtyima* has been fenced in and renamed Mount Taylor by European Americans, symbolizing the material and cultural dispossession of the Pueblo. In this respect, Silko's task would be more like that of an Olinka woman in *The Color Purple,* trying to rebuild the community after having had the village destroyed and the tribe decimated or displaced. It would be unclear whether such a community could be re-created in the absence of that specific place. Her task is similar to Ozick's in that her work seeks a restoration of communal memory. However, the role of the earth in her world means that she cannot imagine cultural memory residing in a text or even simply in a particular community, but must imagine it in a particular place. Thus, in Silko's work the cultural politics of fiction is not readily separated from the real world politics of place. Facing tribal decimation, cultural fragmentation, and the usurpation of the land, Silko's work is an experiment in imaginative remembrance that will allow for the possibility of communal renewal. Her stories trouble the question of whether fiction can adequately recover sacred memories in the absence of a recovered place. Can fiction map an imagined ritual space through which the new realities of twentieth-century America can be incorporated into the life of the tribe? In Silko's hands, fiction retells the tradition in order to make it available for the present, this in the hope that the sacred geography of the Pueblo can be imaginatively reinhabited.

Forgotten Earth, Forgotten People

On a number of occasions, Silko has suggested that when studying philosophy in college she felt an intuitive sympathy with Hegel, as if the basic outlines of the dialectic resonated with her understanding of the Pueblo cosmos.[1] *Ceremony,* her most celebrated work, follows this dialectical pattern, placing the main character, Tayo, between the antagonistic worlds of modernity and Pueblo traditionalism. Although Tayo eventually synthesizes these worlds, at the beginning of the novel he is cast more in the literary tradition of the tragic mulatto. He is the son of an absent, alcoholic Pueblo mother and an unknown white father. Tayo faces the thesis of the overwhelming and self-evident superiority of Anglo modernity as represented in the school, the economic system, and the technology of war. The antithesis is an ineffectual and befuddled traditionalism represented in the old medicine man, Ku'oosh.[2]

Thus, when the novel opens, the consequences of this uneven dialect have already effectively destroyed Tayo's sense of his place in the world. He has just returned from World War II, a war he entered at the urging of his cousin Rocky. While there, he witnessed Rocky's brutal death at the hands of his Japanese guards. Rocky's death and the overwhelming brutality of the war leave Tayo unable to believe in the promises of the American dream that Rocky had represented. At the same time, the secluded world of the reservation seems disconnected from the larger world, its stories and rituals appearing naive and quaint in the face of wars of mass destruction. The following scene suggests that Tayo is between cultural worlds without a coherent relationship to any specific world.

> Tayo didn't sleep well that night. He tossed in the old iron bed, and the coiled springs kept squeaking even after he lay still again, calling up humid dreams of black night and loud voices rolling him over and over again like debris caught in a flood. . . . [The] fever voices would drift and whirl and emerge again— Japanese soldiers shouting orders to him, suffocating damp voices that drifted out in the jungle steam, and he heard

the women's voices then; they faded in and out until he was frantic because he thought the Laguna words were his mother's, but when he was about to make out the meaning of the words, the voice suddenly broke into a language he could not understand. (5)

The many voices here provide no coherent cultural memories which might provide Tayo with some direction and guidance. They are, rather, a hurricane of noise in which Tayo tosses helplessly. Clinically, we might say that Tayo is suffering from post-traumatic stress, but more broadly his condition describes what Peter Berger calls "anomy," a kind of metaphysical homelessness. Berger has suggested that the world construction which every society undertakes and for which religion has traditionally played a vital role is so crucial to individual identity that the loss of one's place in the world feels like the loss of one's self, a nearly unendurable psychic dislocation. With the loss of what Berger describes as "sustaining conversations" carried on by a culture, individuals plunge into an uneasy sense of unreality.[3] "Not only will the individual then begin to lose his moral bearings, with disastrous psychological consequences," says Berger, "but he will become uncertain about his cognitive bearings as well. The world begins to shake in the very instant that its sustaining conversation begins to falter" (22).

In Greek, *nomos* can be both a custom and a habitation, a way of doing things and a place that a culture inhabits. This is a particularly useful term here in that the Pueblo sustain their cultural identity with particular customs, or habits of being, associated with particular spaces of habitation. Tayo has lost a sense of relationship with a particular place. He no longer participates in the sustaining conversations that would allow him to inhabit a world. The chaotic voices destroy one another and leave him silent and alone.

While Tayo's distress has a variety of individual causes, symbolically his homelessness springs from the decimation of cultural imperialism. European Americans and Mexicans have effectively fragmented Pueblo cultural memories and have stolen, divided, or destroyed the land. Thus, they have destroyed both the *nomos* of Pueblo custom and the *nomos* of Pueblo habitation.

In the novel, the most significant means by which Pueblo rituals have fragmented is through the story of enlightenment propagated by the educational system. According to this story, human beings forget their ignorant past for the knowledge of modernity. The educational system embodies this active forgetting by disengaging Native Americans from traditional views of the landscape and wildlife around them. In school cultural aggression wears the thin disguise of useful knowledge:

> The first time in science class, when the teacher brought in a tubful of dead frogs, bloated with formaldehyde . . . the Navajos all left the room; the teacher said those old beliefs were stupid. The Jemez girl raised her hand and said the people always told the kids not to kill frogs, because the frogs would get angry and send so much rain there would be floods. The science teacher laughed loudly, for a long time; he even had to wipe tears from his eyes. "Look at these frogs," he said, pointing at the discolored rubbery bodies and clouded eyes. "Do you think they could do anything? Where are all the floods? We dissect them in this class every year." (203)[4]

The confrontation between the unnamed Jemez girl, the Navajos, and the teacher is a paradigmatic confrontation between two interpretive worlds. On the one hand, the earth is alive, active, possibly vengeful or helpful. On the other, it is bloated, gray, rubbery, artificial, available for dissection and the further expansion of scientific knowledge. Moreover, these stories do not compete on equal footing. Through the institutionalized power structures of the educational system represented in the teacher, one is normal, natural, scientific, rational, truthful; the other is archaic, superstitious, childish, clownish.

Tayo's memory of the school particularizes the master narrative of enlightenment at the center of the educational system.[5] According to this master narrative, humanity has moved from the darkness of primitive fears and superstitions and into the adulthood of scientific knowledge (Jameson, "Realist Floorplan," 373–83). In the United States, the land without history is free for development, the raw material out of which a new self can be made. The land, profane in its materiality, is free for exploitation, free to be made over in our own image for our own cultural, intellectual, economic, and recreational benefit.[6]

In Tayo's life, the most extreme example of this ideology is, ironically, Rocky, Tayo's half-brother, who has died in the war. While Rocky genuinely loves and accepts Tayo, he also represents the Pueblo who believe that the ways of Euro-Americans are superior to the ways of Pueblo tradition. Rocky incarnates the American dream. A successful athlete and student, he agrees with his teachers that traditional obligations to family must be discarded and the individual must strike out on his or her own, in Rocky's case to college, where a football scholarship awaits. He agrees at every turn that Indian initiative and history are worthless in the face of science associated with the larger American culture. Clearly he is one representative of what Richard Rodriguez has called "the scholarship boy," a child who "cannot afford to admire his parents" and who "concentrates on the benefits education will bestow upon him" (49). Rocky becomes something of a model minority, manifesting no palpable regrets about his lost past.

Rocky's life at first appears glorious as Tayo follows him to the army and war in the Philippines. But the glory dims as Rocky becomes a stereotypical Ugly American. Rocky reveals his inhumanity when he chastises Tayo for not participating in the execution of some Japanese prisoners. The execution incapacitates Tayo when he envisions one of the Japanese prisoners as his uncle Josiah.

> So Tayo stood there, stiff with nausea, while they fired at the soldiers, and he watched his uncle fall, and he knew it was Josiah; and even after Rocky started shaking him by the shoulders and telling him to stop crying, it was still Josiah lying there. . . . Rocky made him look at the corpse and said, "Tayo, this is a Jap! This is a Jap uniform!" And then he rolled the body over with his boot and said, "Look, Tayo, look at the face," and that was when Tayo started screaming because it wasn't a Jap, it was Josiah, eyes shrinking back into the skull and all their shining black light glazed over by death. (7)

The same person who cuts himself off from family and tradition sees a human being as a uniform, or even as so much roadkill to be poked at with a foot. Josiah is uncle to both these young men, and so Rocky symbolically destroys his own family in his desire to follow the rules of American success as exemplified in the military establishment. Thus he both fulfills and demonstrates the consequences of modernity's desire for rupture with the past.

Between Past and Future: Traditions for the Present

As I have suggested, the ideologies of modernity embedded in American nationalism, racism, and scientism reconfigure the minds of the Pueblo in Silko's novel, causing them to forget both themselves and the land which sustained the traditional community. In response to this forgetting, Tayo loses his resources for resistance and collapses by default into the apparently self-evident superiority of modernity. Just as Celie's belief in a white male God led her to acquiesce to male domination in *The Color Purple*, Tayo's inability to construct an effective alternative narrative leads him to acquiesce to the apparent superiority of Euro-American reality. He witnesses this superiority everywhere. *Kawaishtyima* is renamed Mount Taylor and reconstructed as a commodity by being fenced in and turned to ranch land. Whites are wealthy. Indians starve, and those who do not starve are alcoholics. At the nadir of Tayo's despair, when he has gone to visit the medicine man, Betonie, and has begun to doubt that even Betonie can help him, Tayo reflects on the apparent helplessness, poverty, and insignificance of native peoples: "[All] of it seemed suddenly so pitiful and small compared to the world he knew the white people had—a world of comfort in the sprawling houses he'd seen in California, a world of plenty in the food he had carried from the officers' mess to dump into garbage cans. [Betonie's] clothes were dirty and old, probably collected like his calendars. The leftover things the whites didn't want. All Betonie owned in the world was in this room. What kind of healing power was in this?" (133).

The loss of cultural memory is more than a lapse of the forgetful brain; it is everywhere embodied out in the material world around him. Representatives of a traditional Pueblo life are few and far between and those who are present seem mostly ineffectual. His grandmother is blind and appears oblivious to Tayo's struggle. She does suggest that the traditional medicine man, Ku'oosh, be summoned, but Ku'oosh seems largely lost in the past, unable to comprehend the psychic devastation that has occurred since the coming of white Americans. Although he performs a ceremony for Tayo, he seems less than confident that his work will do much good:

> "There are some things we can't cure like we used to," he said, "not since the white people came. The others who had the Scalp Ceremony, some of them are not better either."
>
> He pulled the blue wool cap over his ears. "I'm afraid of what will happen to all of us if you and the others don't get well," he said. (39)

To some degree these representatives of Pueblo memory fail because they so easily conform to the master's narrative wherein ethnic, tribal, or other postcolonial peoples are quaint memories of the past rather than effective means of addressing the present. As with Rosa in Cynthia Ozick's story, connection to the past can be destructive or irrelevant if means of bringing the past into a fruitful relationship with the present cannot be found. Over and against their stasis in the past, Silko posits hybrid characters who are able to consume facets of modernity and combine them with Pueblo traditions so that hybrid forms of Pueblo traditions can act effectively in the present. Various characters fill this hybrid role throughout the novel: Josiah, who tries to teach Tayo some of the Pueblo traditions and who tries to develop a cattle herd that will combine the best of Mexican and North American breeds to be adapted to Indian ways on the reservation; Night Swan, Josiah's lover, a Mexican-Pueblo who makes love to Tayo and tries to reassure him that he is playing an important role in a much larger ritual drama. Even Tayo's illness suggests some small degree of personal resistance. Compared to Rocky or the evil character Emo, Tayo seems psychically and physically incapable of supporting the violence of the contemporary world, even if he feels helpless to overcome it. In the war, Tayo sees the Japanese as relatives, suggesting that he has moved beyond a simple identification with tribal others, and, more important, beyond a simple identification with one's own countrymen. This ability to identify with many others suggests that Tayo is a hybrid character in the tradition of Josiah, Night Swan, and others, those who attempt to find a new way of living in the world. Yet he remains without a story that will make his hybrid character effective.

By far the most important hybrid character in the novel is Betonie, the Navajo-Mexican medicine man to whom Tayo finally goes for a ritual healing. Betonie seeks to heal Tayo through stories and rituals that integrate Tayo's contemporary reality with a long tradition of Pueblo memory. Betonie recognizes the necessity of changing rituals to cope with a changing world:

> At one time, the ceremonies as they had been performed were enough for the way the world was then. But after the white people came, elements in this world began to shift; and it became necessary to create new ceremonies. I have made changes in the rituals. The people mistrust this greatly, but only this growth keeps the ceremonies strong.
>
> [My mother] taught me this above all else: things which don't shift and grow are dead things. They are things the witchery people want.

Witchery works to scare people, to make them fear growth. But it has always been necessary, and more than ever now, it is. Otherwise we won't make it. We won't survive. That's what the witchery is counting on: that we will cling to the ceremonies the way they were, and then their power will triumph, and the people will be no more. (132–33)

Betonie embraces adaptation, appropriation, and change. He collects a wild array of modern and traditional detritus in his hogan, organizing them to reflect a ritual universe. As a Mexican-Navajo, he represents the racial crossings of contemporary Native American reality. Such cross-racial and cross-cultural alliances also reflect the ways in which tribal cultures have found points of alliance with tribes formerly considered enemies or who were simply outside the tribal sacred cosmos. Even the ceremony that Betonie performs for Tayo reflects the hybrid character that he is embodying, being a combination of traditional ceremony, storytelling, and practical directives about how to go about living in the world.[7]

One purpose of many religious rituals is to remind people of the basic stories of a community, this in order to carry forward the "sustaining conversations" upon which the sacred cosmos depends. Further, while Peter Berger tends to see traditional religions as alienating human beings from consciousness of their own agency (81–101), many Native American tribes see their rituals as necessary to the maintenance of the order of the universe and, by extension, of their own identities. In short, inhabiting an eternal or sacred cosmos secures the significance of human agency. The people and the land are inseparable.

If this is true, then becoming separated from the sacred cosmos can disable human agency, hurting both the individual and the community. Many religions recognize that persons can become separated from the sacred cosmos, and religious rituals can reintegrate the alienated into community (Eliade 20–65; Brown, "Becoming," 9–20). Tayo has been separated from the stories and practices which might have provided an alternative to the destruction of the war. Betonie's ceremony is designed to integrate Tayo into a form of life in which alternative stories pertain, enabling practices and conversations that sustain a different form of life.

Specifically, Betonie creates a sandpainting that illustrates a story of ritual healing.[8] Tayo sits in the center of the painting, where Betonie has painted the picture of a mythological boy who has been incapacitated by Coyote, a Navajo trickster. Tayo then walks in the painted paw prints of a bear, physically reenacting the boy's original healing. During the ritual, Betonie reaches forward and cuts Tayo's scalp; the flowing blood identifies Tayo with those whom he has killed in World War II. By walking in the bear's footprints, Tayo begins to walk in concord rather than in discord with the Indian world. He is being introduced into the possibilities of a different world, a world in which the story of defeat and destruction can be replaced by other life-giving stories.

This process of engaging Tayo in the kinds of sustaining conversations that would return him to a Native American cosmos continues throughout the second half of the novel. Perhaps most crucially, Betonie provides Tayo with an explanatory narrative that resituates the history of Native American oppression by redescribing "social" and "natural" phenomena as spiritual phenomena. Destructive forces such as war and alcoholism are revealed as forces of "witchery." Tayo's problem is not illness but evil, evil defined as being alienated from others and from the earth:

> Then they grow away from the earth
> then they grow away from the sun
> then they grow away from the plants and animals
> They see no life
> When they look they see only objects.
> The world is a dead thing for them
> the trees and rivers are not alive
> the mountains and stones are not alive.
> The deer and bear are objects
> They see no life.
>
> They fear
> They fear the world.
> They destroy what they fear.
> They fear themselves. (142)

This description of evil extends the Navajo understanding that the essential characteristic of evil is self-interest opposed to others. The selfish person tries to stand apart from the interconnectedness that characterizes the nature of stories in general, and particularly the interconnectedness of the Pueblo peoples (Graulich 10). As Barre

Toelken suggests: "For a person to act as if he had only himself or herself to care for or be concerned about was tantamount to an admission of interest in, or practice of, witchcraft. . . . Those who are thought to be witches are usually characterized by selfishness, acquisitiveness, lack of concern for other family members and for clan relationships" (63).

When Tayo despairs at the dispossession of Native Americans by white Americans and Mexicans, Betonie replies that even this dispossession can be understood within a Native American world. Separateness is first and foremost an Indian problem.[9] Betonie suggests Indian witchery is ultimately responsible for the evils of imperialism, replacing the story of Indian victimization with the possibility of Indian agency. As Betonie says to Tayo, "[We] can deal with white people, with their machines and beliefs. We can because we invented white people in the first place" (139). Such stories about the origins of evil force Tayo to recognize his implication in similar processes and to take responsibility for resisting that evil.

In Navajo traditions, the sandpainting ceremony heals; it has performative power (Brown, "Becoming," 20). Why, then, does *Ceremony* not end when Tayo finishes enacting the part of the boy who is to be healed? Just as Celie's story in *The Color Purple* reaches a narrative climax when she leaves Albert, but then continues its complications, *Ceremony* seems to promise a narrative fulfillment during Betonie's ritual, only to push on into further conflict and complexity. Although the ceremony seems to have accomplished something, it does not seem to have reintegrated Tayo into Pueblo life. Indeed, a section of poetry following the sandpainting ceremony suggests that the process of healing has only just begun, that the blessing is not really achieved. "The rainbows returned him to his home, but it/ wasn't over/ all kinds of evil were still on him" (151).

However, the residue of evil indicates not so much failure as the specific historical situations in which Tayo's ceremony takes place. Sandpainting ceremonies originated in a very different form of life. Like most other religious traditions in the modern era, Indian religious practices have been significantly fragmented into a separate and discrete sphere of activity, largely unrelated to what a person may do with his or her life elsewhere. Sandpaintings may be bought at art auctions, and ceremonial dances may be viewed for the price of a ticket. Such dances or paintings are often beautiful, even meaningful, but they speak to a form of life that exists primarily as a memory rather than a lived practice (Deloria, "Chaos," 259–68).

Therefore, the ceremony that could be performed without reference to the life Tayo has to lead outside the ceremonial context is likely to have more in common with a religion of private experience than Indian traditions. Somewhat like Celie's need to discover ways in which her new ideas about God can be lived out in the world of *The Color Purple,* Tayo must put Betonie's stories into practice. Tayo's problem is not simply that he has not been performing rituals, but rather that the life he leads and the world around him is infected with evil.

Tayo must reimagine the earth and the economic and social practices that have caused him to "grow away from the earth." This effort begins when he recovers Josiah's cattle. Prior to the war, Josiah was the primary person in Tayo's life who sought to find ways of continuing traditions in the modern world, as well as one of the few who actually tried to teach Tayo of Pueblo traditions. In pursuing this dream of a viable Pueblo tradition in the modern world, he developed a hybrid cattle breed adequate to life on the reservation, cattle that would "grow up heavy and covered with meat like Herefords, but tough too, like the Mexican cows, able to withstand hard winters and many dry years" (84). During the war, Josiah died and these cattle were stolen and fenced in by a white rancher, ending that dream. Tayo's search for the cattle begins on Mount Taylor, *Kawaishtyima.* While he is on the mountain, Tayo shows a great ritual respect for the earth and its inhabitants, and Silko's language indicates that the natural world has become an agent as well, sustaining Tayo even as he sustains the earth.[10] The earth itself gradually becomes less a spectacular backdrop than a coagent with Tayo in creating the possibility of a new life.

For instance, some time after Tayo has sprinkled ritual pollen in a mountain lion's footprints, he is captured by employees of the ranch. He only escapes when they discover the mountain lion's tracks and leave to hunt it down. This particular scene reaches a climax when the earth protects not only Tayo but also the cattle and the mountain lion as well.

The snow was covering everything, burying the mountain lion's tracks
and obliterating his scent. The white men and their lion hounds could
never track the lion now. He walked with the wind at his back. It would
cover all signs of the cattle too; the wet flakes would cling to the fence
wire and freeze into a white crust; and the wire he had cut away and the
gaping hole in the fence would be lost in the whiteout, hidden in snow
on snow. Under his feet the dark mountain clay was saturated, making
it slippery and soft; the ranch roads would be impassable with sticky
mud, and it would be days before the cowboys could patrol the fences
again. He smiled. Inside, his belly was smooth and soft, following the
contours of the hills and holding the silence of the snow. He looked back
at the way he had come: the snowflakes were swirling in tall chimneys
of wind, filling his tracks like pollen sprinkled in the mountain lion's
footprints. He shook his head the way the deer shook snow away and
yelled out "ahooouuuh!" Then he ran across the last wide flat to the
plateau rim. (214–15)

Here Tayo becomes the earth, the snow which covers him symbolizing and restoring their connection just as his cut scalp in the sandpainting had earlier symbolized his connection with those who had
been killed in the war. The land "becomes" Tayo through the metaphor of the pollen ritual, caring for Tayo as Tayo cared for the mountain lion, protecting Tayo as Tayo protected both the lion and the
cattle.

This imaginative identification intensifies in Tayo's relationship
with Ts'eh, a figure for the Pueblo *Ko'chininako*, Yellow Woman.[11]
Yellow Woman's role among the Pueblo is as various as the many stories told about her, sometimes simply a legendary tribal woman who
disappears with a mountain spirit, sometimes the mother of war gods,
sometimes a spirit distantly related to the creator, Thought-Woman,
and specifically associated with *Kawaishtyima*. Her role in *Ceremony*
seems most closely linked to the latter of these multiple instantiations.
Ts'eh helps Tayo find the cattle and helps him hide and get away with
the cattle once he has rescued them. Their sexual relationship surely
suggests some kind of human fulfillment, but because Ts'eh is a spirit
responsible for the creation, this imagery takes on larger resonances.
Whereas romantic and erotic love often represents a break with the
past, a necessary separation from and rebellion against the life of the
home that embodies the past, in embracing Ts'eh, Tayo embraces
woman, earth, and Pueblo traditions. This consummation blends the

worlds of human beings, gods, and nature; it also suggests a new connection with the past: "He dreamed he made love with her there. He felt the warm sand on his toes and knees; he felt her body, and it was as warm as the sand, and he couldn't feel where her body ended and the sand began. He woke up and she was gone; his fists were full of sand" (232).

Their lovemaking here is only barely "realistic" and instead acts as the ultimate metaphor for a fully human practice. Tayo is uncertain as to whether he has made love to a human being, a goddess, or the earth, a metaphorical connectedness that represents his entrance into a life world in which these could not be easily separated. Embracing her, Tayo embraces the earth, the traditions of Pueblo peoples, and the community that sustains both.

Ts'eh, like Betonie, guides Tayo into a world that has no separate word for religion, so integrated is the life of the spirit with the life of the world (Brown, *Legacy*, x). Unlike the science teacher who encourages a radical break with the past, Ts'eh teaches Tayo to adapt the traditions of the Pueblo to the present. Unlike the ranchers who use animals as commodities, Ts'eh helps Tayo develop a cattle herd that might live like the deer of an earlier Indian era. Ts'eh teaches him about various plants and their purposes, and she enlists him to gather these plants for replanting in locations that need their particular powers. Ts'eh's practices assume a different stance toward the earth than the cultural systems that had earlier resulted in Tayo's illness. Now in the role of gardeners, Ts'eh and Tayo refoliate the earth: "He would go back there now, where she had shown him the plant. He would gather the seeds for her and plant them with great care in places near sandy hills. The rainwater would seep down gently and the delicate membranes would not be crushed or broken before the emergence of tiny fingers, roots, and leaves pressing out in all directions. The plants would grow there like the story, strong and translucent as the stars" (266).

Tayo has finally emerged from a metaphorical underground darkness into a new creation. According to the origin myth of the Acoma, two Ur-human beings emerged into this world and were taught by *Tsichtinako* how to go about bringing things to life and how to sustain that new life in the new creation. Thus human beings and the gods collaborate in creation and in sustaining creation (Velie 12–28). By extension, cultural memories serve as more than mental constructs. Rather, such memories imply different possibilities. Memories can also be matters of flesh and blood, of cattle and sandpainting, of planting and making love; in short, stories are part and parcel of the making and sustaining of a world.

Earth, Memory, and Apocalypse

At *Ceremony*'s close, Tayo watches from a cliff as his old drinking buddies brutally murder one another. Because he realizes this signifies the end result of witchery, he resists the impulse to join the mayhem by murdering the most hateful character in the novel, Emo. By resisting the path of violence and bloodshed and pursuing the path of peace and creation, Tayo has truly completed his ceremony and is reintegrated into the life of the tribe.

Following his harrowing experience in the desert, Tayo tells the elders of the tribe of his encounter with Ts'eh. They respond:

> A'moo'ooh, you say you have seen her
> Last winter
> up north
> with Mountain Lion
> the hunter
>
> . . . .
>
> They started crying
> the old men started crying
> "A'moo'ooh! A'moo'ooh!
> You have seen her
> We will be blessed
> again. (269–70)

On the one hand, this event surely signifies Tayo's reintegration into the tribal cosmos. His personal story has been made possible through the stories that preceded him, and his retelling to the elders means that his story is now part of the tribal story, ensuring that the stories upon which the tribal culture depends will continue.[12] Thus, "We will be blessed again."

This chant suggests the teleological dimension of Silko's story, a dimension that calls for hope and anticipation, a provision for the time being until the blessing is fully realized. To say "We will be blessed again" is a joyful recognition, but one pointed toward the future. In this sense, too, Silko's book is like Betonie's sandpainting ceremony, a beginning rather than an end. This provisional quality is reiterated in the closing poem of the novel.

Whirling darkness
started its journey
with its witchery
and
its witchery
has returned upon it.

Its witchery
has returned
into its belly.

. . . .

It has stiffened
with the effects of its own witchery.

It is dead for now.
It is dead for now.
It is dead for now.
It is dead for now. (273–74)

The witchery is dead, at least so far as the narrative of the book is concerned. But the witchery is only "dead for now." Because the creation is ongoing, there will be other occasions for witchery to show its face and other occasions for witchery to be countered, other novels to be read, rituals to be performed, creations to be undertaken, memories to be recalled.

This irresolution at the end of *Ceremony* also suggests the degree to which this story of personal healing only anticipates a larger communal reality. Tayo's healing is far along, but the community's healing is only anticipated. Also left unresolved is the ambiguous status of the land that was seen as the primary issue in the first place. Indeed, so pronounced is Tayo's individual healing as the centerpiece of the story that Bonnie Winsbro can read the story primarily as a story of "individuation" without much reference to community or land at all. As she puts it, "Through choice and will, then, Tayo locates and assumes an identity capable of sustaining and empowering him" (108). Relationship to tribe and place, which are necessary components of personal healing, seem left mostly to the side of this equation. Tayo's story becomes one of psychic and largely internal reorientation rather than the reestablishment of the intricate, interpenetrating web of relationship between memory, place, community, and individual. Thus the ambiguity at the end of *Ceremony* speaks not simply to Pueblo views of the persistence of evil, but also to the sense that the whole story has yet to be told. If we are left with "The evil is dead for now," the natural question is, "What happens next?"

In Silko's case what happens next is *Almanac of the Dead*. In many respects *Almanac of the Dead* continues and intensifies the concerns of *Ceremony* to such an extent that it is possible to think of the two books as companion pieces. In both, Silko is concerned with the question of relationship to the earth. In both, she considers the earth an active principal rather than an inert object to be used. In both she is concerned with the interactions between various cultural groups brought into contact through the migrating forces of imperialism and modernity: Mexicans, Pueblos, other Native American tribes, Anglos, African Americans mix together in a stunning array of violence, cultural uncertainty, and psychic disintegration.

Despite these similarities, *Ceremony* and *Almanac of the Dead* are so different in both form and tone that it is sometimes difficult to imagine the novels being written by the same author. Commenting on this disparity, Silko spoke about the reaction of various readers to the two texts: "At signings, people would come and buy three or four copies of *Ceremony* when they bought *Almanac*. And they said things like, 'I give these out to my friends.' I was so embarrassed . . . Then I've also felt real protective of people, thinking, Oh no, these dear little people that love *Ceremony*, what's going to happen to them when they get sucked into the maelstrom of *Almanac*? In Seattle a man told me he thought *Almanac* was affecting his sanity, and finally I just said, 'I hope it won't harm you, or if you think it is, then stop'" (Perry 331–32).

In part, the difference between the two books seems to be not unlike Richard Wright's decision to cut through the rather easy way a white readership embraced *Uncle Tom's Children* and celebrated Wright as the latest "Black Author of the Year." In response he wrote *Native Son*. Similarly, *Ceremony* is often a reassuring novel, while *Almanac of the Dead* has the feel of an author rejecting the role of gentle and noble savage.

But beyond the peculiarities of Silko's authorial personality, one reason for the blunt force of *Almanac of the Dead* is that Silko directly addresses the issue of ownership of the land that *Ceremony* introduces but leaves to the side in the final instance. Tayo can feel good about planting a variety of ritual plants in the arid New Mexican landscape, but it is unclear that this activity will do much to address the massive deforestation of the South American rainforests, the metaphorical goring of the earth in the process of mining for uranium, the depletion of water resources in the Southwest through massive population growth in the urban centers such as Phoenix. While Tayo might successfully breed a hybrid cattle herd following Josiah's suggestions, it is unclear how the success of that herd and the concomitant economic success of Native Americans will mean much of anything except their integration into the political economy that is destroying the land around them. How will Tayo's remembered stories be able to do much to reorganize the sacred cosmos of the Pueblo people, given the political realities of divided borders and the economic realities of divided land?

The apocalyptic tone and the sometimes nauseating events of *Almanac of the Dead* can partially be described as moving beyond *Ceremony*'s small triumphs, translating them to an international scale. This difference is illustrated on the inside covers of *Almanac of the Dead*. The illustration is a map of the so-called southwest "border" between Mexico and the United States, but the map questions the narrative of national forgetting that the apparently settled geographical spaces of the nation-state inscribe. If national memories are always narratives of remembering and forgetting, then what the map of the U.S.–Mexican border forgets or leaves out is the history of Native American suffering and struggle, a history of resistance that both Mexico and the United States would like to erase. Indeed, one important event in the novel is the trial and execution of a Cuban revolutionary who, through his own take on Maoist revolution, has dismissed tribal stories. He is executed because he has forgotten tribal histories.

Silko's map undermines forgetting, as well as our traditional notions of thinking through novels, by having these borderlines overlaid with names of the novel's characters and criss-crossed with lines that indicate the movements of characters—and drugs and weapons and pornography—back and forth across the border. Thus, without forgetting national stories or the political and social realities called the United States and Mexico, Silko destabilizes this geography by showing how the stories of the Southwest disfigure such borders. The movements and actions of people through time and space are more important than the bounded notions of the nation-state. Indeed, she titles the map "Almanac of the Dead: Five Hundred Year Map," suggesting that the memory of Indian resistance forces us to rethink the nature of national narratives as well as national boundaries, to say nothing of the nature of space. As she writes in one corner of the map: "Sixty million Native Americans died between 1500 and 1600. The defiance and resistance to things European continue unabated. The Indian Wars have never ended in the Americas. Native Americans acknowledge no borders; they seek nothing less than the return of all tribal lands."

This is, to say the least, a bold and confrontational declaration. The balance of *Almanac of the Dead* attempts to envision the kind of world in which such a declaration can be seen as coming to pass.

It is not my purpose in these concluding pages to provide a "close reading" of *Almanac of the Dead,* as I have done with *Ceremony.* Indeed, it is not clear that this chaotic novel lends itself easily to close reading at all, unlike *Ceremony* with its more integrated vision. Rather—putting aside Indian revolutions in Mexico, drug trade and addiction, prostitution, sexual decadence, and illicit trade in human organs harvested from murdered homeless people—I want to focus on two aspects of religious memory that are relatively central to the novel: the fact of the Almanac itself, and the Giant Stone snake. These two elements illuminate the particular problems of memory, place, and ritual that are central to *Ceremony* and to Silko's vision as a whole.

The almanac referred to in the novel's title is an ancient written document that recorded the future of the Indian peoples of the Southwest. The original version of this document disappeared, symbolically eaten by its first guardians, who memorized the stories before eating the leaves of the book. These guardians passed the stories down through the generations until they were recorded in notebooks by the grandmother of two of the novel's central characters: Zeta and Lecha. As Zeta and Lecha read, piece together a narrative, and transcribe the stories, the events in the almanac appear to be taking place, signaling the end of this particular era of history and a restoration of Indians to the land.

The notion of the almanac clearly shares a number of issues taken up in *Ceremony.* The almanac is a peculiar kind of memory which envisions the interpenetration of past, present, and future. Silko has suggested that in sympathy with her Pueblo heritage, she imagines time as an ocean rather than a river. She imagines herself living within a time-space in which past, present, and future are close at hand and intermingled.[13] Thus, the events and memories of five hundred long years ago have relevance for the contemporary Chiapas uprising in Mexico and for the building of the atomic bomb in New Mexico.

Further, the almanac continues the tradition of hybrid mixing evident in *Ceremony*. On the one hand, of course, that there is a *written* almanac at all testifies to the incorporation of European elements into the Pueblo world. Indeed, the almanac is said to be written on stretched horsehide using a technique learned from the Spanish. Moreover, the imagery of consumption and retranscription suggests a commerce between traditionalism and modernity. The original guardians literally eat the original almanac, making it a part of their bodies. However, they only do so after having memorized the original. By passing the stories down, the almanac figures a movement from oral to written to oral again. Finally, in the present time of the book's narrative, the almanac has been retranscribed and is being reread and in this sense rememorized by the characters Lecha and Zeta. Like Betonie, who used whatever was at hand to keep the rituals alive and effective, the almanac represents the possibility of hybrid forms being incorporated into ritual memory.

The great stone snake is likewise a figure of memory. Explicitly described by Silko's illustration as a "spirit messenger," the snake represents the return of Native American conceptions of life to the world of the Southwest. In the passage that follows from the end of the novel, Sterling—a character similar to Tayo in that he is somewhat separated from tribal traditions—goes to visit the stone snake: "Sterling had thought that probably the strange sandstone formation had been lying there for hundreds of years and no one had noticed it. . . . But Aunt Marie and the others had pointed out the sheep camps nearby and the road that passed within a hundred yards of the giant stone snake. . . . No way had they overlooked a sandstone snake thirty feet long! Overnight, the giant stone snake had appeared there. The old folks said Maahastryu had returned" (761).

The spirit snake is described in the transcribed notebooks of the almanac as a sacred spirit that lived in a lake that was destroyed by the people. As a result, the sacred spirit left the people. But the snake also speaks to the people in a prophecy:

> *I have been talking to you people from the beginning*
> *. . .*
> *What I have told you has always been true.*
> *What I have to tell you now is that*
> *this world is about to end.* (135)

This apocalyptic prophecy is played out throughout the book and is re-inscribed at the end of the novel when Sterling finally understands and accepts the significance of the stone snake: "Sterling knew why the giant snake had returned now; he knew what the snake's message was to the people. The snake was looking south, in the direction from which the twin brothers and the people would come" (763).

It is difficult to replicate the ominous tone of this ending, but consider that the people to the south are Indians undertaking revolution in Mexico, those who have executed Bartolomeo for forgetting tribal histories and who have aided the self-destruction of the Mexican elite during the course of the novel. The snake's message to the people is one of imminent apocalypse that entails the destruction of the European inhabitants of the land and the return of ancient lands to the ancient people.

This apocalyptic tone is different from *Ceremony* but also has its roots in the seeds that *Ceremony* metaphorically sowed. It differs because Silko has clearly given up on the pacifist vision so central to rituals of *Ceremony*. Tayo could not engage in violence against anyone because violence fed the bloodlust of the witches. The apocalyptic vision of *Almanac of the Dead* seems to suggest that the destruction of Europeans is the only means of reestablishing the ritual cosmos of the Pueblo and other native peoples. This destruction must include violence if necessary. Thus, without suggesting that violence and revolution are glorious and romantic, *Almanac* generally endorses the Chiapas uprising, the execution of Bartolomeo, and other forms of revolutionary activity that promote the return of the people from exile.

As surprising as this vision is, its apocalypticism seems inevitable given the contours of memory, place, and ritual as found in *Ceremony*. Derek Phillips has pointed out that one critical component of contemporary communitarian theorizing is the value of place. As Phillips puts it, "[Communitarian writers] see shared locality or place as having a unique community-engendering power. In a genuine community, they emphasize, people's affiliations are not the sort that are formed entirely voluntarily or broken at will. A common locale helps assure that people's ties to other community members are to some extent unwilled and nonvoluntary" (12).

As with Alice Walker's "earth-centered" spirituality, this notion of place is notable in its lack of specificity. The communities envisioned by Alisdair McIntyre and Robert Bellah require an actual place—the Internet cannot be a community, nor can the modern corporation—but just about any place on earth will do equally well. Even for Cynthia Ozick, who might be expected to place some special emphasis on the "place" of Israelite homeland, identity and community are less dependent on a specific place than upon specific memories and specific people. By contrast, Silko's community demands a particular orientation to a particular land.

Therefore, for Silko, religious memory has more far-reaching consequences than for the other writers that I have examined so far, precisely because memory calls for the reconfiguration of more than one's mind and one's relationships. Tayo's memories of a different life provoke the desire to live in a particular way in a particular place. However, this is only possible if something else is put to death besides the evil that exists within Tayo's psyche. The fences must come down, and not only metaphorically within Tayo's mind and spirit; they must literally be torn down to the degree that they deface Pueblo cultural identity on *Kawaishtyima*. Pueblo culture requires not only sustaining conversations but also a sustaining place. The restoration of a particular habitation requires not only the decolonization of the Pueblo mind but also the decolonization of the Pueblo earth and all that such a revolutionary rhetoric implies.

Thus, the dreadful apocalypticism of *Almanac of the Dead* traces its lineage to the remembered earth of *Ceremony*. The tending of tender plants and memories in *Ceremony* requires the destruction of all that eviscerated land and memory in the first place. The horrific scene toward the end of *Ceremony*—in which the witches, Emo and Pinkie, torture and finally kill their compatriot Harley—is more than simply emblematic of the way evil feeds on itself. It is a necessary precondition for the healing of the land that Tayo undertakes with the help of Ts'eh.

This necessary violence is carried to its conclusion in the apocalyptic vision of *Almanac of the Dead*. Despite their apparent differences, the impulses of violence and restoration in the two novels imply one another, in impulses born first in the colonial violence that sought to suppress memory in the name of desire, in impulses carried forward in the desire for memory that seems inscribed in the land itself. With somewhat less hope and a great deal more fear than in *Ceremony*, the great stone snake at the end of *Almanac* points, like the synthesis of Hegel's dialectic, toward a future in which these antithetical poles of desire and memory can be resolved.

5

Chanting the
Descent Lines

MAXINE HONG KINGSTON'S *THE WOMAN WARRIOR*

Toward the conclusion of *Almanac of the Dead,* Silko has a
character repeat an often invoked division between religions
Western and religions Native American.

> Yoeme said even idiots can understand a church that tortures and kills
> is a church that can no longer heal; thus the Europeans had arrived in
> the New World in precarious spiritual health. . . . The Europeans had
> not been able to sleep soundly on the American continents, not even
> with a full military guard. They had suffered from nightmares and fre-
> quently claimed to see devils. Cortés's men had feared the medicine
> and the procedures they had brought with them from Europe might
> lack power on New World soil; almost immediately, the wounded
> Europeans had begun to dress their wounds in the fat of slain Indi-
> ans. (718)

Consonant with the general vision of *Ceremony* and of *Almanac
of the Dead,* Silko characterizes cultures based on assumptions concerning the nature of the earth. The material world and the spiritual
world are the same thing, and the failure of Europeans to perceive
this homology indicates the gulf between Native American and
European modes of viewing the world.

This division is common to many Native American writers. In *God Is Red,* Vine Deloria posits a Native American spiritual outlook that is completely at odds with Western and particularly Christian views of the world. Gerald Vizenor invokes a similar division based on a distinction between a Native American emphasis on balance between good and evil and a Western desire to eradicate evil (Bowers 44). The tendency in such discourse is to envision difference as absolute opposition.

However, my argument throughout this book has suggested that difference is not absolute. These ethnic women have appropriated various aspects of dominant Western discourses, sometimes transforming them, sometimes using them alongside ethnic religious traditions in an uneasy compromise. Ozick uses postmodern literary techniques and elements of the romantic literary tradition in order to engage and revivify a Judaism that she feels is opposed to both postmodernism and romanticism. Walker critiques Christianity's sexism but seeks to transform its discourses in a way that provides continuities between traditional forms and newer, less clearly Christian forms of African American culture. Similarly her use of African American vernaculars transforms the epistolary novel, creating what Henry Louis Gates calls a "speakerly text," a hybrid form that invokes oral tradition through the means of the Western novel (*Signifying* 239). Even Silko's *Almanac of the Dead,* with its parodic impulse and encyclopedic themes of conspiracy and destruction, might find space on the generic shelf beside Sterne's *Tristam Shandy,* Pynchon's *Gravity's Rainbow,* or Delillo's *White Noise.* Silko checks the tendency to divide the world into Indian and non-Indian through Betonie's pragmatism in *Ceremony.* Betonie appropriates those elements of European culture that he finds useful and transforms the religious culture that he has inherited from the Pueblo and Navajo.

This same tension between division and transformation is evident throughout the work of Maxine Hong Kingston, reaching a paradoxical extreme as Kingston herself insists vehemently that her work is thoroughly American, even while the "Chinese elements" of her works lead reviewers to emphasize their exotic "foreignness." On the one hand, cultural traditions common to China, the land of Kingston's parents' birth, are far removed from Western modes of religious speculation. Indeed, dominant religions such as Buddhism, Confucianism, and Taoism deemphasize a world of spirits and gods in favor of an ethical world of discipline and self-transformation. Even popular religion, with its panoply of spirits, gods, and ancestors, seems most concerned to maintain one's relationship to the social world.

At times, the differences of Eastern religions leave Kingston uncertain of how to establish the relationship between the two cultures. Late in her second memoir, *China Men,* Kingston remembers the elaborate safety drills that sustained the domestic anxieties of American schools at the height of the Cold War.

> For the Korean War, we wore dog tags and had Preparedness Drill in the school basement. We had to fill out a form for what to engrave on the dog tags. I looked up "religion" in the American-Chinese Dictionary and asked my mother what religion we were. "Our religion is Chinese," she said. "But that's not a religion," I said. "Yes, it is," she said. "We believe in the Chinese religion." "Chinese is our race," I said. "Well, tell the teacher demon it's Kung Fu Tse, then," she said. The kids at school said, "Are you Catholic?" "No." "Then you're a Protestant." So our dog tags had O for religion and O for race because neither black nor white. Mine also had O for blood type. Some kids said O was for "Oriental," but I knew it was for "Other" because the Filipinos, the Gypsies, the Hawaiian boy were O's. Zero was also the name of the Japanese fighter plane, so we had better watch our step. (276)

The young Kingston's position between worlds suggests the difficulty of understanding the role of religion in cultural and political life. As with Silko, the tensions between these worlds are realized forcefully in the public school system, symbolic of all political and social institutions committed to nation-building. The school registers ethnic religions in ways that amputates them from their originally encompassing cultural lives, an amputation that figures China as an absence for both Kingston and official public culture. Incorporated into the discursive world of the dog tag, Chinese religion becomes something other than itself, something more easily identifiable within the classificatory systems of the United States. Yet the category also maintains an aura of threatening otherness.

On the one hand, "the Chinese religion" as conceived of by the mother and partially understood by Kingston confronts modernity and is partially reconfigured in the process. Because it is "Oriental" and "Other," the child's religion carries with it the stigma attached to dominant Western views of Asian Americans. Here, religious categories exclude Kingston from the dominant cultural discourses of the West. In being marked as different she becomes an enemy. However, such categories also inadvertently provide for new alliances and traditions. With the Koreans, Filipinos, Gypsies, and Hawaiians she is marked with an "O," the sign of the Japanese Zero. On the one hand, the zero sustains an outsider status. On the other hand, it provides a source of potential strength and threat as those who do not fit the acceptable categories form new alliances to undermine the social ideologies that exclude them.

Throughout Kingston's work she oscillates between these poles of oppression and opportunity as she works through the relationship of Chinese religion to America. This is especially evident as she thinks through issues of gender. On the one hand, Chinese religions are a source of gender oppression since they have justified brutality against women. Thus the cultural emphasis on individual rights and opportunities in America enables Kingston to resist her oppression as a woman. On the other hand, American individualism can lead to an emotionally destructive isolation that separates her from others and from the past. Thus, Chinese emphases on relatedness and community enable her to critique the most extreme forms of American individualism. Through the course of this chapter I will examine Kingston's effort to find a hybrid balance between traditions of relatedness and the artistic and personal need for self-expression. Through writing she transforms both the ethnic traditions of the Chinese and the American culture in which she lives.

Religion and Relatedness

Kingston's attempt to define Chinese religion at school reveals the ways in which religious categories can structure a sense of belonging. By categorizing in this way, of course, the school establishes order among the students by a perceived relatedness: this group is one kind of people, that group is another kind. As Kingston's memory makes clear, this kind of categorizing can work in devastating ways to the degree that it Orientalizes the Asian school children as Other and threatening.

On the other hand, the mother also uses Chinese religion to maintain a sense of group identity, what we might call a sense of order generated, or imposed, from within. Almost all religions include some emphasis on connectedness to others or to a world of the spirit. The word "religion" is itself rooted in the Latin for "binding together." Nevertheless, there are vast differences in the nature and degree of this connectedness. At the one pole many Protestantisms conceive of the religious life as a singular relationship to God, with connections to others being a residual benefit of that primary relation. By contrast, in traditional China, relation to others through the practices of ancestor reverence, social obligations to elders, and obligations to the state is almost the entire content of religion, with God or the gods subordinated to ethical concerns.[1] Somewhat like Tayo in the Pueblo cosmos, but to an even greater extent, the traditional Chinese person knows herself by her position in relationship to others in a carefully elaborated system of obligation. In answering questions concerning personal identity, the traditional Chinese person would think first of the identity of others.

Mary Stange has suggested that in many cultures women emphasize relatedness in their ways of perceiving themselves. Therefore, women's autobiography tends to displace the self who is the putative subject of the narrative. Given this conjunction of gender and ethnicity, it is not surprising that we find Kingston telling her story in *The Woman Warrior* by telling the stories of others. Indeed, the novel opens with her mother's voice telling the story of another woman living thousands of miles from Kingston's own town of Stockton, California. Such emphases in the story contribute to what Kingston calls the misreadings by white reviewers of her work, because these stories seem to emphasize Kingston's connection to an exotic Chinese otherness.[2]

However, whatever the benefits of community as an abstract ideal, relationship can also be deeply oppressive. One thinks immediately of the value of relatedness in *The Color Purple,* where Celie lives in community at the end of the novel with Shug, Albert, and others of her family. This redeemed community, however, is countered by the brutalizing relatedness of the first two-thirds of the novel. In practice, relatedness has often meant relatedness to men, and in Chinese America this has meant being subject to the male family line. In old China the economic, cultural and ritual relationship of women to men was one of horse to rider. To note only one example, peasant fathers were known to sell daughters into slavery or prostitution. From birth, through slavery, prostitution, brokered marriages, and unpaid labor, women were commodities bought and sold in a gendered market (Hill Gates 799–832). In the Chinese American immigrant community these practices necessarily changed, but the fundamental relationship of subservience remained. If arranged marriages were no longer the norm in America, Kingston could still imagine in her memoir that her parents would sell her to the neighborhood idiot. If slavery is no longer the norm, Brave Orchid's endless work in the family laundry images the thousands of Chinese American women who sweat out twelve- and sixteen-hour days in laundries and garment factories, all to the profit of others.

This hierarchical relationship which denies the autonomy of women is, of course, common enough in Western societies. But within the Chinese American community, one of the most important ideological factors constructing that hierarchy is the residual effect of a Chinese religious cosmology that places the highest values upon village, family, and ancestors. In Chinese tradition, knowing your village and being known by your village provided you with what John Berger describes as the nomos, a spiritual location in time and space by which you knew yourself.[3] So central are the village and one's immediate neighbors that Lao Tze envisioned Utopia as a village in which "the next place might be so near at hand that one could hear the cocks crowing in it, the dogs barking; but the people would grow old and die without ever having been there" (Tsai 34). Relatedness in such a setting extends not simply to one's immediate family members or to one's neighbors, but indeed through the memories of the village into the distant past, fixing one's identity in relationship to the villagers who have shaped the village life in the past.

Thus, relatedness, in the Chinese context, is shaped primarily by the Confucian imperatives of filial duty. Unlike European American emphases that expect children, especially male children, to strike out on their own and "cut the apron strings," as the proverb puts it, traditional Confucianism expects the son to remain loyal to parents and village. More important for my own purposes, the woman was expected to remain loyal to the man. Under Confucianism, "[a] well-regulated hierarchical state depended on the maintenance of three principal bonds of loyalty and subordination, that of minister to prince, son to father, and wife to husband" (Ling 3). Thus the perfectly ordered society depended partially on the restriction of female freedom. The hierarchical order of family life reflected the hierarchical order of social life, all of which Confucianism imagined as reflecting a perfect, hierarchical Celestial Order.[4] This doctrine was ultimately codified as the Three Obediences and The Four Virtues: "The Three Obediences enjoined a woman to obey her father before marriage, her husband after marriage, and her eldest son after her husband's death. The Four Virtues decreed that she be chaste; her conversation courteous and not gossipy; her deportment graceful but not extravagant; her leisure spent in perfecting needlework and tapestry for beautifying the home" (Ling 3).

The network of familial obligation that Confucian political religion demanded bound a woman to the priority of her male kin just as her bound feet hobbled her at home. These family bonds extended not simply to the first and second generation but, through the popular religion of ancestor reverence, into the distant past as well (Yang 29). Yang points out that since ancestor rites served to cement the social structure of the kinship group, "family members occupying unimportant organizational positions such as those remaining unmarried and those under the age of twelve at the time of death were comparatively ignored" (47). While Yang does not mention women specifically, their position depended primarily on their relationship to the males of the kinship group, and therefore their position in the ancestral hierarchy was relatively marginal as well. Indeed rituals honoring ancestors usually honored the father's line of descent, meaning in practice that parents without sons would be less well-cared for in the life to come than would their more adequately blessed neighbors (Overmeyer 24).

Given this background, Kingston is less sanguine about the possibilities of relatedness than Silko is in *Ceremony* and is less interested in the direct recovery of a disrupted tradition like that envisioned by Cynthia Ozick. More like Walker in her troubled recognition of the oppression of women by tradition, Kingston's imagination often recoils from China, emphasizing its brutalizing aspects ("Reservations About China"). The opening of *The Woman Warrior* suggests less that Kingston finds her voice through connection to Chinese traditions than that familial obligations are all but disabling to her imagination. The mother's story enjoins silence rather than imaginative expression.[5] Unlike Walker, Kingston treads cautiously in her mother's gardens, seeing them as a locus of gendered violence and silencing in the opening lines of the text: "'You must not tell anyone,' my mother said, 'what I am about to tell you. In China your father had a sister who killed herself. She jumped into the family well. We say that your father has all brothers because it is as if she had never been born'" (3).

On the one hand, Kingston's narrative form values relatedness. The story opens not with Kingston's voice, Kingston's story, or Kingston's perspective, but with the story of an aunt told by her mother, Brave Orchid. To know Kingston we will have to know a variety of other stories told by a variety of other persons, all of which mark Kingston's relatedness. Her identity as daughter, citizen, and, perhaps most important, as author will be quite complex, known only in and through its obligation to others.

But this opening tale is not the benign remembrance of an unfortunate black sheep in the family line. Rather it is also a method by which "China" and the "Chinese family," as they are represented in the voice of the mother, attempt to fix Kingston's identity, attempt to pin her to her place. Brave Orchid's cautionary and bloody tale of organized ritual violence against women justifies that violence and then identifies the aunt's experience with the possibilities of Kingston's life. The aunt, whom Kingston calls the "No-Name Woman," has been guilty of having a child who could not have been her husband's, though the biological fact may be due to rape, incest, or infidelity. By disturbing the clarity of the family lines, and by bearing a female child in time of famine, the aunt and her family are punished by the villagers. They wreck her home and raze her fields. Distraught, the aunt kills herself and her child by leaping into the family well. After telling Kingston this story, her mother makes its ideological design clear: "Don't let your father know that I told you. He denies her. Now that you have started to menstruate, what happened to her could happen to you. Don't humiliate us. You wouldn't like to be forgotten as if you had never been born. The villagers are watchful" (5).

The story brings the obligations of kinship to bear on Kingston's young life. Moreover, Kingston's silence emphasizes and secures this obligation, as does the threat of having to endure the silence of others. Kingston's father denies the aunt and by implication will also deny Kingston. The villagers live only in the mother's story, but this makes them no less effective in securing the child's obedience.

The villagers do not represent an eccentric or marginal social set, but rather an entire spiritual and political cosmos which parent is communicating to child. Kingston calls this cosmos "the roundness," a term which in practice seems quite similar to Berger's concept of the *nomos*.

> The frightened villagers, who depended on one another to maintain the real, went to my aunt to show her a personal, physical representation of the break she had made in the "roundness." Misallying couples snapped off the future, which was to be embodied in true offspring. . . . [A] family must be whole, faithfully keeping the descent line by having sons to feed the old and the dead, who in turn look after the family. The villagers came to show my aunt and her lover-in-hiding a broken house. The villagers were speeding up the circling of events because she was too short-sighted to see that her infidelity had already harmed the village, that waves of consequences would return unpredictably, sometimes in disguise, as now, to hurt her. (12–13)

The villagers are hurting the aunt literally by destroying her house. But more to the point, they are hurting her sense of identity by cutting her off from the rest of the village, from the system of relationships through which she could know who she was. Far from finding oneself through asserting independence, independence is to be feared, resulting in the utter loss of self. The aunt's isolation generates Kingston's own fear of being cut off from her family. Imagining the aunt who has transgressed the mores of her village as a romantic rebel, Kingston sees her finally lost to the world, dominated by an absolute fear: "She turned on her back, lay on the ground. The black well of sky and stars went out and out and out forever; her body and her complexity seemed to disappear. She was one of the stars, a bright dot in blackness, without home, without a companion, in eternal cold and silence. An agoraphobia rose in her, speeding higher and higher, bigger and bigger; she would not be able to contain it; there would be no end to fear" (14).

The obligations of social and familial ties compound the horrors of this story in that such obligations continue into the afterlife. The metaphysical system in which the family cares for the spirits of dead ancestors ensures, perversely, that the aunt's punishment will never end. The family refuses to remember her in the afterlife. Her isolation will continue: "People who can comfort the dead can also chase after them to hurt them further—a reverse ancestor worship. The real punishment was not the raid swiftly inflicted by the villagers, but the family's deliberately forgetting her. Her betrayal so maddened them they saw to it that she would suffer forever, even after death. Always hungry, always needing, she would have to beg food from other ghosts, snatch and steal it from those whose living descendants give them gifts. . . . My aunt remains forever hungry. Goods are not distributed evenly among the dead" (16).

Such tales of perpetual punishment and need fix Kingston within a negative and restrictive economy of relatedness. The mother's comment on Kingston's menstruation implies this economy and suggests that Kingston's own behavior had best exist within such restricted possibilities for women. While Kingston did not inherit a specific place that would be analogous to Lao Tse's Utopia, she surely did inherit the ideologies of relationship upon which that Utopia was based. The villagers continue to be watchful over a young American girl with no memories of China, their gaze passed through generations and across space and time by a mother using the instrument of story. Through stories passed down from generation to generation, stories that bind person to person, present to past to future, Kingston is bound into a certain social space which she cannot violate lest the mythic villagers visit her with the horror visited upon her aunt. Without descendants to honor her in death, the aunt exists as a memory of horror, tradition serving to silence rather than enable Kingston's imaginative life.

Of course, the profound loyalty to specific place envisioned by traditional Confucianism and Chinese popular religion has necessarily fractured as succeeding generations of Chinese Americans have grown up without the firsthand memory of China and within a cultural system that attaches relatively less value to specific place. In remembering her aunt, Kingston also imagines her own placelessness as a Chinese American woman. On the one hand, being American excludes her from the traditions of China. On the other hand, she is subject to the traditional exclusion of Chinese from full participation in American life, an exclusion that was felt most acutely by Chinese women.[6] However, she also feels this sense of not belonging to a village because the ideology of unmoving loyalty to place is almost nonexistent in the dominant discourses of American life. The gruesome results of such loyalty in Kingston's work have lead many critics to insist that Kingston resists the claims of her relatives and an ancestral past by affirming her American identity.

Indeed, as a child of Chinese immigrants, growing up in Stockton's Chinatown, attending both public and Chinese schools, speaking Chinese at home and English at school, Kingston has a certain practical flexibility and freedom that her aunt could never imagine, a mercurial self that has much more to do with America than the position of women in traditional China. When her mother reminisces yet again about "their" village back in China, Kingston says, "I could not figure out what was my village" (45). During a confrontation with her mother she opposes her abilities as a student in an American system to the low expectations that Brave Orchid has of her as a Chinese girl.

Such moments in the novel seem to situate *The Woman Warrior* as an affirmative drama of assimilation. Upon this reading, Kingston's troubling over America merely signals the passing inadequacy of the immigrant experience. Accordingly, Kingston aspires to be the American Adam (or Eve), aspires to an individual identity that is opposed to every other identity. On this reading, relatedness is the fundamental liability which Kingston must overcome. Negative reviewers see this as racial or ethnic self-hatred. More positive reviews sometimes write the drama of the book as the unfolding of Kingston's life from Chinese ignorance to American strength; the Woman Warrior is the American self.

These readings, however, minimize the fact that Kingston does not easily identify Stockton, or America, as the place in which her spiritual identity and purpose can be located and maintained. Kingston struggles to free herself not only from a conservative ethnic heritage but also from the fragmentation and displacement which modern social systems exacerbate, especially for women. Not simply oppressed by ideologies of "roundness," Kingston the American child also recognizes with distress that she has no "roundness" at all, no place in which she fits, no *nomos* in which her identity is easily defined. Growing up in an America that imagines Asian Americans to be Charlie Chans, Dragon Ladies, or Fu Manchus, Kingston experiences America as a source of pain, confusion, and restriction. Explaining that the Chinese ideogram for "I" has several complex strokes, she remembers as a school girl that she could not understand the American "I" (166–67). She is judged by the American educational system to have a zero IQ (183). She tries desperately to be "American feminine" so she can get dates (172). She tries to speak alone in class but fails (166). She gets fired from a job by a racist employer (49). Her American life is described as a "disappointment" (45).

Indeed, Kingston's effort to become the independent self represented by the upright and independent "I" often fails traumatically. As with Tayo in *Ceremony,* this failure is brought to the fore in Kingston's education, which seeks to separate individuals from ethnic communities. As a young child in the public school system she is expected to stand alone and read aloud, a pedagogical enactment of the American value of individuality (166). This lonely effort to achieve an adequate speech contrasts starkly with her experience in Chinese schools, where speaking was not a problem because no one was expected to speak alone: "[At Chinese School] we chanted together, voices rising and falling, loud and soft, some boys shouting, everybody reading together, reciting together and not alone with one voice. . . . The girls were not mute. They screamed and yelled during recess, when there were no rules; they had fist-fights" (167).

Given Kingston's representation of the oppressiveness of the Chinese American subculture, especially toward women, this scene is striking in its empowerment of women precisely within the confines of that culture. The geographical space of the Chinese school and Chinatown frees Chinese Americans to be themselves precisely because their individuality is not at stake as it is in American society as a whole.

The violence implicit in an excessively individualistic imagination manifests itself when Kingston asserts herself violently over and against a weaker *doppelganger* in the bathroom of the Chinese school. Taking on the persona of the street tough kids she sees in public school, she abuses a silent Chinese American girl who reminds her too much of herself. The violent encounter culminates in the following harangue:

> And you, you are a plant. Do you know that? That's all you are if you don't talk. If you don't talk, you can't have a personality. You'll have no personality and no hair. You've got to let people know you have a personality and a brain. You think somebody is going to take care of you all your stupid life? You think you'll always have your big sister? You think somebody's going to marry you, is that it? Well, you're not the type that gets dates, let alone gets married. Nobody's going to notice you. And you have to talk for interviews, speak right up in front of the boss. Don't you know that? You're so dumb. Why do I waste my time on you? (180–81)

On the one hand, Kingston's persona takes on the most extreme forms of individualistic behavior. The failure to be independent and self-assertive in the American economy means being unemployed and unmarried, thus blocking two means by which women in America are imagined to have some form of material security. Ironically, in order to achieve an economically secure "relationship" with boss, husband, or boyfriend, Kingston feels the need to assert herself violently against others, to stand out in the gendered marketplace of the United States. Like the slave girls in China who perform anxiously so that they might be bought by a "good" master, Kingston's America sets her against other women, especially Asian women, as she works desperately to be accepted by a male master. Kingston's fears about not making it in the solitary world of American culture are projected on the silent and defenseless smaller child. Rather than being a sign of Kingston's gradually growing strength of character, the extremity of the violence and the helplessness of the victim critique the values represented in a hyper-individualism wherein women compete with one another for job and spouse. Like Rocky kicking a corpse who looks like his uncle in Silko's *Ceremony*, Kingston's violent abuse of a defenseless girl suggests not strength but weakness, not growth but violence and destruction. The scene does not affirm the "American I" but rejects it. The text seems to judge the young Kingston. Immediately following the beating she has given her innocent *doppelganger*, she falls ill and silent for a number of months, as if taking the defenseless child's impotence upon herself as punishment.

This hesitation before aspects of American conceptions of self signals Kingston's critical thinking about American culture. Such thinking comes even more to the fore in later works like *China Men* and *Tripmaster Monkey*, texts that, in part, examine the consequences of racism for the culture and identity of the Chinese American male, even while also claiming America for Chinese American men and women. Clearly the collection of such themes in her work prevents one from easily affirming the notion that Kingston is uncritically embracing American values at the expense of egregious stereotypes of China and Chinese Americans.

Chanting the Descent Lines: Toward a Hybrid Self

Given the ambivalence toward both America and China expressed in *The Woman Warrior*, an ambivalence that is perhaps even more pronounced in some other works, Kingston faces questions of identity not unlike those of Tayo in Silko's *Ceremony* or the characters in the

Chanting the Descent Lines

works of Cynthia Ozick. Like those characters, the past cannot be abandoned, but it is even less clear how the past can be made to speak to the present. If anything, Kingston is even more ambivalent about this problem because many aspects of the present are far superior to the past. How can Kingston shape a sense of her position in the world as a Chinese American woman that will not simply give assent to the past? How, at the same time, can she manage to avoid simply abandoning the past for a world of isolation and loneliness, cut off from family and traditions that have nurtured others through the generations? Like the other authors I have examined thus far, Kingston proceeds by appropriating specific traditions from her mother's memories and reenvisioning them to make them useful for her in her American present.

The clue to Kingston's appropriation of Chinese religious traditions comes midway through the text as Kingston imagines her mother's life in prerevolutionary China. In one vignette, Kingston's mother agrees to exorcise a ghost that has been frightening her fellow students in a Chinese medical school. After Brave Orchid's successful battle, her friends chant her descent lines to remind her of who she is, thereby recovering anything of herself that has been lost in the battle with the malevolent spirit: "The students at the To Keung School of Midwifery were new women, scientists who changed the rituals. . . . A relative would know personal names and secrets about husbands, babies, renegades and decide which ones were lucky in a chant, but these outside women had to build a path from scraps. No blood bonded friend to friend. . . . [They] had to figure out how to help my mother's spirit locate the To Keung School as 'home'" (75).

On the one hand the chanted descent line reflects the emphasis on relationship common to Confucianism and popular religion. On the other hand, this tradition has been changed because it no longer fixes Brave Orchid in relationship to her husband and father and instead organizes her life in relationship to her present, especially a present shared with other women. The resonances with Silko's Betonie are remarkable here since Betonie also changes the rituals and is not bonded to Tayo by blood. By chanting an ancestral heritage, Brave Orchid's friends recall her to herself. But this act is more than a blind orientation to the past that ancestral reverence can sometimes become; rather, the students creatively reimagine this ritual in order to call Brave Orchid to her specific present: "The calling out of her real descent line would have led her to the wrong place, the village. These strangers had to make her come back to them. They called out their names, women's pretty names, haphazard names, horizontal names of one generation. They pieced together new directions, and my mother's spirit followed them instead of the old footprints" (75–76).

Much like Betonie, the women in the Chinese medical school live on the cusp of history where two worlds meet, where two different horizons have begun to fuse (Hart 58–60). On this cusp, a naive traditionalism cannot serve these "new women," and so must be reimagined to bring Brave Orchid to herself in the present rather than losing her in a misty nostalgia for the past.

In this story we can see a figure of Kingston's entire text. On the one hand, she is related to China, even as her mother is from a particular village. On the other hand, just as her mother has left that village and has made her way by immense personal effort to become a physician, Kingston's identity is not determined so much by her relationship to China as by the voice she achieves as an author in the United States. Yet, Brave Orchid does not simply abandon the values implicit in village life since being in relationship remains central to identity. Now, however, she has arrived at a position with a "new village" of other women like herself who are learning both traditional Chinese medicine and new Western medical techniques. The chanted descent line is a tradition of reverence for relationship, but it is a tradition reconfigured to meet Brave Orchid's necessarily changed circumstances. Similarly, Kingston's embrace of America is not a simple rejection of China, but rather what is usable from China is reconfigured to meet Kingston's circumstances as an American.

We can hear this chanting of new Chinese women as a metaphor for Kingston's practice as writer. The text is a chanted descent line, a ritual fiction in which Kingston pieces together a line of descent filled with women's names and women's stories. These names give Kingston her own address in time and space as an American woman of Chinese ancestry. These stories give her the imaginative grounds from which she weaves stories that ultimately insert themselves into the reader's history, providing for a new and different imagination. This descent line is not automatically given by a conservative heritage of ancestor reverence. Nor is it automatically empowering. Rather it must be

pieced together like one of Alice Walker's quilts or Leslie Silko's ceremonies, making the usable past fit the present needs of a Chinese
American woman. Just as Walker and Silko found that their own traditions had to be faithfully revised in order to counteract evil within
and without that tradition, so also Kingston revises traditions of reverence for ancestors to counteract the gendered and generational hierarchies that she experiences in America.

Just as the women chanting Brave Orchid's descent line emphasize
revision, the stories included in Kingston's text emphasize revision.
Revision of Chinese stories, and bringing them into relationship with
American stories, is necessary if Kingston is to locate herself and
other Chinese American women in space and time. To fail to revise
would be to lose oneself. Indeed, one of the most unnerving stories
in the book is of just such a woman who loses herself in coming to
America: Kingston's aunt, Moon Orchid. Under the influence of
Brave Orchid's imaginative world that seems stuck in China, Moon
Orchid embodies the unmediated transference of Chinese traditions
and Chinese stories to an American context. Moon Orchid's home is
China, and she is unable to construct a new descent line, a new story
that would place her home in America. She loses herself because she
has lost the context in which stories can make sense: "Moon Orchid
had misplaced herself, her spirit (her 'attention,' Brave Orchid called
it) scattered all over the world" (156–57). Brave Orchid furthered
her sister's unhinging by imagining that Chinese traditions, especially
traditions concerning family responsibility, could be hauled intact
across the Pacific Ocean. She assumes naively that the traditions of
China can be dislodged from their historical and cultural context and
transferred willy-nilly to postwar America, forgetting or never seeing
that she herself has been a mediating figure who has had to adjust
and change her own life. Moon Orchid ends her days in an asylum,
speaking to other women who clearly do not understand a word she
is saying, but whom she imagines as relations. If the No Name Aunt
is a cautionary tale concerning young women who bring shame on
their families and villages, Moon Orchid is a cautionary tale concerning those who cannot manage to find a way to bring old and
new contexts into contact with one another.

Clearly Kingston runs this risk since much of the text shows her
alienation from various contexts, whether Chinese, Chinese American,
or Euro-American. At the extreme, she remembers this alienation in

her being bedridden and silent for months following her assault on the silent Chinese girl in the school bathroom. However, Kingston finds within her mother's stories and her mother's practices the resources for developing a new sense of relatedness, one that does not bind her to specific places or to silence, but one that allows for a newly empowered voice.

Indeed, the irony of Brave Orchid's complicity in Moon Orchid's descent to insanity is that Brave Orchid is the most obvious and necessary person to be included in Kingston's line of descent. Who Kingston would be without her mother is unimaginable, and not simply because of the facts of biology. In many ways Brave Orchid is a precursor: the first to seek a profession for herself as a midwife, the first to make the trek between the cultures of America and China, the first to have a life independent of men.

Thus, just as the No Name Aunt figures and precedes Kingston in another less helpful way, Brave Orchid is the most significant "ancestor" through which Kingston comes to understand and name herself. Brave Orchid supplies the words and stories that give Maxine Hong Kingston an identity and provide a ground for her own activity as a storyteller. Brave Orchid mediates an ancestral and imaginative line by first telling the stories that Kingston constantly retells: "Night after night my mother would talk-story until we fell asleep. I couldn't tell where the stories left off and the dreams began, her voice the voice of the heroines in my sleep. . . . At last I saw that I too had been in the presence of a great power, my mother talking-story. . . . She said I would grow up a wife and a slave, but she taught me the song of the warrior woman, Fa Mu Lan. I would have to grow up a warrior woman" (19–20).

Those who precede us set our destiny in motion, a concept symbolized by Kingston's understanding of her work as an author. She acknowledges that she continues rather than originates stories, that "the beginning is hers, the ending, mine" (206). The "ending" which Kingston assigns to herself is a powerful act of identification, translation, and completion. Without this act of translation, Kingston runs the risk of becoming like her aunt Moon Orchid who fell under Brave Orchid's spell.

Ironically, then, Brave Orchid authors Kingston's authorship. If she communicates a great deal of Chinese sexism to her American daughter, she also equips her daughter powerfully with mythic stories to create an identity for herself and other Chinese American women. She even goes so far, at least in Kingston's uncertain childhood memories, as to cut Kingston's frenulum in order that she might be able to speak many languages, move between many worlds. Kingston calls her own work as an author "talk-story," the term used to describe Brave Orchid's continual storytelling. Kingston figures this identification with her mother poignantly at the end of the chapter devoted to her mother.

> She got up and turned off the light. "Of course, you must go, Little Dog."
>
> A weight lifted from me. . . . She has not called me that endearment for years—a name to fool the gods. I am really a Dragon, as she is a Dragon, both of us born in dragon years. I am practically a first daughter of a first daughter.
>
> "Good night, Little Dog."
>
> "Good night, Mother."
>
> She sends me on my way, working always and now old, dreaming the dreams about shrinking babies and the sky covered with airplanes and a Chinatown bigger than the ones here. (108–9)

Kingston and Brave Orchid are both women warriors in their own ways, despite differences and conflicts and antagonisms. The daughter draws strength and inspiration from the mother's precedence. The text suggests this symbiosis in the final sentence, where it is impossible to identify whether the two dependent clauses refer to "She," Kingston's mother, or "me," Kingston herself. Earlier in the chapter both were described as old, both were described as working always in a harsh American economy. One told stories of shrinking babies and another remembered them and retold them for an American audience. One told stories of airplane formations in the Sino-Japanese War and the other dreams them, reimagining in a memoir the nightmare of war she could not have experienced. One dreams of a Chinatown that is in fact China while another dreams of a Chinatown that will allow her to be at home in America. The syntactic ambiguity does not mark an ambiguity in Kingston's relationship with tradition, but is rather her positive identification with tradition as she marks it with her own accent. Kingston is her mother's voice, chanting the descent line of which she is both inheritor and creator, fulfilling the familial obligation to make sure that memories of her foremothers will not be neglected.

Still, if Kingston is her mother's voice and is telling her mother's stories, those stories have been altered by their new context, where they flow from the tip of Kingston's pen. For instance, given the repressive identification which Brave Orchid makes between Kingston and the No Name Woman early in the book, we might expect that Kingston would reject this identification and assert herself over and against the villagers embodied in her mother's stories. Instead, Kingston embraces the identification, an embrace seen even formally in the manner in which she weaves together the story of her aunt with her own biography, imaginatively leaping across years and oceans so as to give the impression that we are reading the story of a multiple protagonist who is both Maxine Hong Kingston and the No Name Woman. Rather than standing over and against her aunt, Kingston receives her aunt in order to say her own name, in order to tell her own story. This embrace does not signal Kingston's acquiescence to her mother. Like the women in the medical school, she must form her own line, tell her own story in order to arrive at a "home" in America. Rather than a simple occasion for repetition, the mother's story allows for more storytelling, for reinterpretation that may alter practices that oppress women. Kingston provides several such reinterpretations, first seeing the aunt as victim rather than transgressor: "Women in old China did not choose. Some man had commanded her to lie with him and be his secret evil. I wonder whether he masked himself when he joined the raid on her family. . . . His demand must have surprised then terrified her. She obeyed him; she always did what she was told" (6).

On this reading of the mother's story, the aunt epitomizes the woman's place in Chinese tradition. But that very tradition is shown to be self-contradictory since, by following the Confucian principles of obedience to males on which "roundness" depends, the woman destroys the roundness and herself. By obeying men, the No Name Woman threatens the stability of family lines. By insisting on the domination of women, the "roundness" of tradition feeds upon itself like the snake who devours its own tail. Kingston's remembrance critiques patriarchy. Implicitly, for communities to achieve the kind of peace and stability to which the roundness aspires, they will have to rid themselves of the imperative to dominate women.

However, Kingston does not assert herself over and against community or relatedness in any absolute sense, this even despite her fear of the villagers and her "reservations about China." ("Reservations" 67–68). Rather, she rejects their injunction to silence and submission in order to participate in and perpetuate the traditions of remembrance. In the process her transgression calls the tradition to its best self. Rather than forgetting the past entirely, Kingston asks that all of the past be remembered, including her aunt. Thus, later, when Kingston remembers her aunt as romantic rebel or as a pitiful victim, she is not so much denying the importance of family and community as she is calling her family and community to a more just future. Kingston takes the traditions of ancestor remembrance and plays upon them to remember her aunt, who by now has become a metaphor for those whom both Chinese Americans and Americans as a whole have tended to forget. By remembering her aunt, by calling her name as a part of her own, Kingston gives her aunt an imaginative life that had been refused her by the family's silence. Indeed, Kingston says that her writing is the devotion of pages of paper, a kind of origami offering to the spirit of her dead aunt (Warrior 8). Kingston recognizes a responsibility to the forgotten dead, and in so doing embraces the very traditions which have been oppressive. That embrace renews them and in the process begins to transfigure the communities of which she is a part.

This process of revision and identification continues throughout the book as Kingston constructs her descent line. Since the Chinese American female "I" is made up through a series of remembrances rather than through a single stroke of the pen, Kingston affirms the strongest possibilities of the No Name Woman and moves on to other identifications with forebears who may aid her in other ways. Given the unsettling fact that the aunt's life ends in death, Kingston can hardly rest easily with an ancestor whose creative possibilities end in self-destruction. The aunt's death is a fundamental loneliness, a fundamental denial of human community which ancestor reverence seeks to image and instantiate.

Thus Kingston goes on to "recall" or chant the name of Fa Mu Lan, mythic woman warrior. This identification is formally even more complete than with the No Name Woman. As presented in the novel, Kingston is Fa Mu Lan. As the legendary woman warrior, Kingston is raised by gods in the mountains and trained in the ways of warfare. She seeks vengeance for her family against a corrupt emperor and against the robber barons of her own village. She is warrior, wife, mother, daughter, fulfilling the Confucian expectations of familial piety while going beyond them as protector of her people. Kingston imagines herself being recognized as the apotheosis of Chinese female possibility: "My mother and father and the entire clan would be living happily on the money I had sent them. My parents had bought their coffins. They would sacrifice a pig to the gods that I had returned. From the words on my back, and how they were fulfilled, the villagers would make a legend about my perfect filiality" (45).

But legends are not easily brought to bear on the humdrum of everyday life. Immediately following the section quoted above, Kingston leaves a section of white space in her text, as if to graph the immense gulf between herself as legend in her own mind and herself as woman in the day-to-day world of the United States. The text continues with Kingston's assertion, "My American life has been such a disappointment" (45). The powers and possibilities of the imagination do not seem adequate to the problems of the world in which Kingston must somehow learn to live. The enemies which destroy her daydreams are not simply Chinese expectations for women but also urban developers and city planners who tear down her parents' laundry. They are racist businessmen who hold the power of life and death, or at least employment, over a Chinese American female barely able to speak up in her own or others' defense. Oppressors on every side who make the likelihood of her reliving Fa Mu Lan's story in the United States seem extremely slim indeed.

But the problem is not Kingston's inadequacy in comparison to the legendary Fa Mu Lan, a figure with powers that only a child could wildly imagine possessing (Kingston, "Mis-readings," 57). Kingston is not a Chinese woman at all, but an American of Chinese ancestry who has to make sense of that imaginative ancestry in an American context. To identify with Fa Mu Lan naively would be to chant a descent line that leads Kingston not to her home but to a China she has never seen and can never experience. She needs to translate the story so that Fa Mu Lan can tell Kingston something about her own situation as an American.

Kingston makes this translation by suggesting that she and the swordswoman are analogous, not by virtue of magic or warlikeness, but in their devotion to others and in their use of language as a means of remembering and protecting those others. The swordswoman's parents had carved words on her back so that even if she died she would carry in her body the story of the injustice done to them. This bloody image is a concentrated metaphor for Kingston's work as a writer. The words on the warrior's back are precisely her parents' stories, her parents' words about the village history. Thus her body is inscribed within a history of others and she carries those others with her in words. Kingston too is a woman of words, a wordwarrior who has been inscribed by others, most specifically by her parents and the Chinese Americans of Stockton. Like the woman warrior, she carries these words forward into new and different contexts, seeking justice not only for herself but for the people whose words she is. As she says of the woman warrior, "What we have in common are the words at our backs." To be a warrior in this context is not to be the solitary gunslinger of American legend, but rather the preserver and defender of a community. Whereas Clint Eastwood comes to and leaves a dusty Western town as the stranger/savior, Kingston and Fa Mu Lan fight their battles as faithful familiars of traditional communities.

Throughout this chapter, I have emphasized the manner in which Kingston revises Chinese religious traditions associated with relatedness and the remembrance of the past in the hope of creating a more just Chinese American community. But as an imaginative memoir written, received, reviewed, studied, and talked about in America, *The Woman Warrior* also imaginatively re-creates America. The traditions of the Chinese American community question dominant modes of understanding in America as a whole. To say that Kingston is her mother's voice marks a Chinese debt of child to parent, and in marking that debt Kingston also puts many Western notions of subjectivity, individuality, and authorship into question. If Kingston is her mother's voice, then Brave Orchid is also the voice of others who precede her and coexist with her in time and place. These many voices themselves, remembered and reenacted, are the agents of the text. In Western culture, authorship images the independent human being creating *ex nihilo* in the quiet chamber of study or library. Kingston's representation of the scene of her own writing at once critiques this solitary subject and reestablishes the authority of human agency by showing the dependence of agency upon others. For instance, she discusses her depiction of the confrontation between Moon Orchid and her unfaithful husband: "In fact, it wasn't me my brother told about going to Los Angeles; one of my sisters told me what he'd told her. His version of the story may be better than mine because of its bareness, not twisted into designs" (163).

The lines of descent by which Kingston constructs her sense of authorship become very complicated indeed, moving horizontally between siblings, vertically between mother and daughter. The telling of tales is always an inherited event, not one in which authorship and therefore solitary identity can be easily established. But neither does the human agent disappear into the self-referentiality of text. Rather, story precedes storyteller in the mouths of others, these others being the very ground of the storyteller's possibility.

Of course, Kingston does tell stories which focus on her self-conception and on her role as a Chinese American woman in the United States. However, were we to read this as traditional autobiography or novel or other narrative, we would expect the direction and flow of the plot to be one in which the main character reaches some form of final knowledge that would establish him or herself as an independently realized person, tragic or heroic. Dimmesdale recognizes and reveals himself as chief of sinners. Maggie dies. Augustine picks up and reads. Horatio Alger gets his riches. Since we have not had an independent protagonist, but rather a collectivity with which Kingston identifies, this narrative logic is dispersed. While Kingston's life story focuses the many stories she has retold and embellished in the course of the text, the very fact of the multiple stories and personae that make up Kingston suggests the impossibility of the climactic moment in which she would be revealed as the solid and solitary character of her own story, unique and apart from others and from the past. Such a moment would betray rather than fulfill the collective character of the story Kingston has heretofore been telling. Instead, Kingston tells yet another story she has inherited from her mother: the tale of Ts'ai Yen, a Chinese woman captured and held by the barbarian hordes of the north. One night this woman hears the barbarians singing and playing flutes, reaching endlessly for an impossibly high note, a note finally found and held, "an icicle in the desert" (208).

An icicle in the desert is an impossible contradiction, something that melts away before it can be imagined. As a single note in a song, it stands as a nearly impossible ideal, and as a barbarian note, the woman can hardly feel its beauty without the pain of loss. The note, and the longing for the note by the barbarian musicians, and the profound nostalgia and longing it provokes in Ts'ai Yen—this entire structure of feeling—demonstrate Kingston's utopian longing to resolve the contradiction between self and others that current cultural systems tend to promote. On the one hand, the note can be imagined as a metaphor for the American "I." Solitary, aloof, alone, a note so high that if held by itself it surely becomes a shrill and deafening shriek, just as a person alone, without a village, is most surely heard in the isolate shriek of the madhouse.

But the American "I" does not stand alone as an obelisk before which Kingston worships. Rather, it is simply another stroke added to Kingston's Chinese American identity. Ts'ai Yen's note is not sounded alone but rather within the larger context of notes that make up a perfect melody. Kingston sounds her self within the collective context of her life as an American woman of Chinese ancestry. She places the important moment of individuality within a historical heritage that stretches imaginatively to the first Chinese men who helped build America, and back through her mother's imagination to mythic Chinese times and places. Like Ts'ai Yen, who created Chinese songs from barbarian melodies and rhythms, Kingston's song mediates between her different histories, singing songs about her diverse ancestry, to create a new song that reimagines the Chinese American's place within America.

In so reimagining, in so remembering, she reconstructs America as well. Kingston's newly constructed descent line does more than tell her own place in time and space; it even further makes the past, her own past and the past of others, live in a new address. Kingston's novel as collective memory, as ancestral remembrance, as chanted descent line, is read by many who are not Chinese Americans. Thus her memories are spoken into vastly different cultural arenas, ones which have often had little use for historical or familial memory. In this sense, *The Woman Warrior* lays claim to America. In it Kingston lays claim to the imagination of American readers as a whole and lays this claim for the memories of her family and of Chinese America.

CONCLUSION

Religion, Literature, and
the Web of Memory

Throughout *The Woman Warrior,* Maxine Hong Kingston's primary metaphors work against many of our common understandings of not only self-identity but of religion and literature as well. An icicle in the desert is an oxymoron in the strictest sense, a violent linking of two things we would rather keep apart, calling to mind other hybrid anomalies in Kingston's work: an individuality that exists together with others, a present that does not exist in opposition with the past, a voice made up with the voice of others, a tradition that is altered without losing connection to its past. Chanted descent lines suggest an understanding of religious ritual much at odds with the grand visions of narrative coherence that religions often see in themselves, and also at odds with the even more grandiose vision of philosophical "Religion" that believes it can melt every particular human difference to a fundamental purity, discarding the incident of human place and time as so much cosmic slag. Kingston's images also speak against the notion of literature common to the modernist canon that has formed so much of our thinking even to the present; this is no literature of the verbal icon, of the self-consistent and purified whole existing in an impossible space apart from the particularities of human existence in time. Rather, these images are images of the contrary and changing realities of the street. Here is the way religious traditions and literary texts work for people who live without the luxury of time to form a universal vision.

These images of literature and religion as hybrid forms are useful figures for the work of all the writers taken up in this book. Consciously or unconsciously all these writers address religious traditions to and through literature, and in the process they discover the ways in which traditions themselves can bend and be remolded without breaking. Traditions reveal themselves as having less the stony logic of a philosophical edifice and more the practical delicacy and stubbornness of the spider web, plunging here and there to make itself in the context of the moment, as if from air. A good thing this, since in the logic of stones the larger crush the smaller into insignificance. It is also the logic of stones that they are not easily reshaped to fit the practical needs of the moment. These practical needs are the things to which these writers have addressed themselves. Thus Cynthia Ozick fills out her stories with images and anecdotes pasted together across millennia, reminding her readers to remember and not forget. Similarly Alice Walker grabs hold of what is useful in the Christianity she inherited in order to find a place for the women that Christianity has typically disregarded. Leslie Silko creates new ceremonies in the pages of a book, drawing not only from Navajo and Pueblo and other Native American sources, but also from Hegel, Flannery O'Connor, and James Wright. All of these writers, along with Kingston, chant new descent lines that translate memories and traditions to create a continuity between past and present, even while they use the new resources of the present to redeem the past.

In many ways I hope that this image of the spider web is an apt metaphor for the method I have tried to follow in this book. The connections between the authors are various and pragmatic, having the logic of the spider web rather than the architectonic logic of the skyscraper. The differences in their literature and their religions will not allow them to be reduced to a single foundation that we might call "Religion" or even "Ethnicity." Neither can they be treated discretely as belonging to separate ethnic or literary traditions. Like the points of connection in a web, they share too much. Similarly, their work suggests that the important connections between the disciplines of literary studies, religion, history and gender studies cannot be ignored. While any single one of these fields provide useful points of entry into the work, without the contact with other fields a point of strength and understanding will be lost.

The image of the spider web, of course, suggests all the strengths and precariousness of the project at hand, both in this work and in the work of the authors I have examined. Nothing is easier than brushing aside a spider web. As I have suggested, the possibilities envisioned here remain hopeful rather than triumphalist. Ozick's audience remains forgetful. It is unclear that Walker's Celie can find a way to translate her domestic utopia to the everyday realities of working women in the twenty-first century. Like Kingston's Aunt, Moon Orchid, some women really do go crazy under the pressure of ethnic and gendered expectations, this despite the most fervently chanted descent lines. Religion no doubt sometimes still seems like a pointless enterprise given the evil that Silko envisions in a book like *Almanac of the Dead*. Nevertheless, if the cultural memories sustained by religion sometimes seem ephemeral and easily destroyed, they remain annoyingly persistent and difficult to forget. Memories and traditions change and stumble, but they go on, providing points of resistance to those who would forget cultural difference. Like spider webs, they come out at night. They are there in the morning.

NOTES

Chapter 1. Beneath the Table: Religion, Ethnicity, and American Literary Studies

1. Anthologies focusing on discrete ethnic literatures do a significantly better job of including substantial numbers of works related to the religious traditions of the ethnic group. *The Norton Anthology of African American Literature*, *The Riverside Anthology of African American Literary Tradition*, and the early anthology of Native American literature, *The Remembered Earth*, are particularly good examples. Indeed, it is fair to say that literary criticism that focuses on a single ethnic group has done a relatively better job of discussing religious traditions in relationship to culture. The problem becomes most acute in works that attempt to be multiethnic or multicultural in approach. Religious particularity falls by the wayside in favor of other principles of organization or analysis. Part of my assumption in this book is that religions and ethnic groups do not live in discrete spheres separated from one another, and so the attempt must be made to look at ethnic cultures together to identify points of convergence and divergence.

2. Alongside Asad, Bernard McGrane's *Beyond Anthropology*, examines the imperialism inherent in anthropology's description and analysis of tribal religions.

3. On the significance of community in ethnic literature, see Bonnie TuSmith. My sense is that TuSmith takes too little account of the ways in which associating community with ethnicity is a romantic myth, and she takes too little account of the ways in which encounters with modernity have created ethnic communities as mixed or hybrid social traditions. Nevertheless, her emphases on the communal values of American ethnic groups provides a valuable correction to the lamentations concerning individualism found in writers like Robert Bellah. For the degree to which religious studies may be merely a disguised form of Protestantism, see Talal Asad and Carl Raschke.

4. Winsbro seems to replicate Raymond Williams's sense of the nature of the individual in bourgeois societies: "'[I]ndividual,' which had once meant indivisible, a member of a group, was developed to become not only a separate but an opposing term—'the individual' and 'society'" (Williams 12).

5. George Lipsitz has suggested that counter-memory is a dominant narrative strategy in many pop-cultural forms, and in particular in novels by marginalized groups. Somewhat to the side of my own concerns, Lipsitz emphasizes the degree to which counter-memory resists myth—and I would assume by some extension, then, also resists religion. Yet given that the dominant myths of post-Enlightenment Western cultures have largely forgotten or excised the specifics of ethnic religious traditions, we can see those traditions providing for counter-memories to dominant stories, alternatives that are not so much idiosyncratic or individuated but cultural and communal. In this specific narrative sense, religious traditions provide for imaginative transcendence of the given master narratives.

6. This, it seems to me, is part of the assumption behind Jane Tompkins's work in *Sensational Designs*. See especially 122–46.

7. The degree to which Silko, or other Native American writers like Paula Gunn Allen, should be uncritically received on this score is a matter of debate. While Pueblo society is clearly matrilineal, it is not so clear that matrilineage always avoids patriarchal modes of domination. Indeed, in a recent film on Pueblo history, the narrator emphasizes that contemporary society is destroying the Pueblo because it is taking women "away from the home" that had always been their domain (Walsh).

8. Raymond Williams defines the residual and the emergent in the following manner: "The residual, by definition, has been effectively formed in the past, but it is still active in the cultural process, not only and often not at all as an element of the past, but as an effective element of the present. Thus certain experiences, meanings, and values which cannot be expressed or substantially verified in terms of the dominant culture, are nevertheless lived and practiced on the basis of the residue—cultural as well as social—of some previous social and cultural institution or formation. . . . Thus organized religion is predominantly residual, but within this there is a significant difference between some practically alternative and oppositional meanings and values (absolute brotherhood, service to others without reward) and a larger body of incorporated meanings and values (official morality, or the social order of which the other-worldly is a separated neutralizing or ratifying component). . . . By emergent I mean, first, that new meanings and values, new practices, new relationships and kinds of relationship are continually being created" (Williams 122–23).

Chapter 2. Disruptive Memories: Cynthia Ozick and the Invented Past

1. For some of Updike's comments about things ethnic, see "Bech Meets Me," *Picked-up Pieces*, 10–13, and "One Big Interview," 493–519 (see particularly pages 505 and 507). Some of Updike's anxieties were fueled by his sense that a Jewish cabal at *Commentary* was out to get him. Updike's ongoing clash

with *Commentary* editor Norman Podhoretz and his stable of writers culminated in *Bech: A Book* (Knopf, 1970), a not too subtle skewering of what Updike took to be the Jewish literary establishment at the time.

2. This narrative is most exhaustively and convincingly presented by Louis Harap in his suggestively titled literary history, *Into the Mainstream*.

3. Louis Harap has questioned Ozick's narrow understanding of authentic Jewishness (*Mainstream* 167). Harap's tendency to cast the net wide is more common among historians of Jewish-American literature, and he is therefore right in suggesting that Ozick is idiosyncratic on this score. Moreover, Ozick's general conception of ethnicity does not demonstrate the complexity of more recent theorizing about the cultural manifestations of ethnicity. Nevertheless, it seems to me that Ozick is more acute than Harap in her analyses of the consequences of acculturation for religious traditions. If her views are idiosyncratic among literary historians, they resonate remarkably with a number of Jewish theologians and historians, as I will show in a moment.

4. My assertion of the significance of memory to Ozick is not unique. For a particularly interesting reading, see Finkelstein's *Ritual of New Creation* (72ff). My interpretation of Ozick differs from Finkelstein's and others in the attention given to the historical situation of Judaism in America and in my reading of the past as fantastic invention in Ozick's work.

5. "Be careful not to make a treaty with those who live in the land; for when they prostitute themselves to their gods and sacrifice to them, they will invite you and you will eat their sacrifices. And when you choose some of their daughters as wives for your sons and those daughters prostitute themselves to their gods, they will lead your sons to do the same" (Exod. 34:15–16). "Do not intermarry with them. Do not give your daughters to their sons or take their daughters for your sons, for they will turn your sons away from following me to serve other gods, and the LORD's anger will burn against you and will quickly destroy you" (Deut. 7:3–4).

6. These lines reflect the tension American Jewish intellectual and spiritual leaders have felt since the creation of the state of Israel. If the great eschatological hope of Judaism in the Diaspora has been to be "next year in Jerusalem," why have so many Jewish Americans opted not to go? Ozick's position seems similar to those held by Maurice Samuel and others in the group that Carole S. Kessner has called "The Other New York Jewish intellectuals," men and women who did not—like Trilling, Kazin, Howe, and others—eschew their Judaism for a humanist liberalism but chose to live in a tension between two worlds.

7. Joseph Lowin is more generous to Puttermesser here, suggesting that the utopia is achieved through "the golem's energy" and "Puttermesser's moral stance" (133). The utopia fails not because of any flaw in Puttermesser's design but because "It is in the nature of utopias that they do not last" (131). My own reading is closer to Victor Strandberg, who emphasizes the flaw in Puttermesser's

embrace of Hellenism. While I do not emphasize the split between Hellenism and Hebraism, this conflict would be one feature of the problems with memory that I am detailing in this essay. For descriptions and analyses of the golem legends, see Gershom Scholem's *Kabbalah* (351–55) and his essay "The Golem of Prague and the Golem of Rehovot" (*Messianic Idea* 335–40). In brief, "The golem is a creature, particularly a human being, made in an artificial way by virtue of a magic act, through the use of holy names" (Kabbalah 351).

8. Although she is without the political radicalism of someone like Doctorow, her practice seems to be somewhat similar to Jameson's evaluation of Doctorow's historicity. Jameson suggests that by using the tools of the postmodern cultural dominant, Doctorow is able to recall the reader to a sense of history, or at least the sense of its absence (Stephanson 19–20). Similarly, Ozick's use of history is not so much a simple pastiche or historical simulacrum—which it would have to be if she denied historical rupture entirely. Rather, Ozick deploys postmodern techniques to create a rupture in the surface of the present, a rupture which emphasizes the absence of the Jewish past as the critical problem with the Jewish present. Jameson goes so far as to call Doctorow's procedure a kind of negative theology, an intriguing term given my discussion of the religious roots of Ozick's practice. Still, for Jameson this practice is absolutely negative, pointing to the necessity of history by emphasizing the absence of history on the postmodern scene. While Ozick's procedure is largely negative in this sense, her work also attempts to communicate tradition, however fragmentary that attempt may be.

9. This idea is scattered throughout Rubenstein's text, but see especially his two chapters entitled "The Unmastered Trauma" (83–122) and "Modernization and the Politics of Extermination" (123–39).

10. Victor Strandberg reads Stella and Persky somewhat differently than I do, suggesting that they are embodiments of what he describes as the "l'Chaim principle" of Jewish life, a principle that values the present moment. Thus they stand in nearly unreconcilable opposition to another principle of Jewish life, the preeminence of memory that I have been emphasizing in this essay (139–51). My reading gives more credence to Rosa's denunciations precisely because Stella and Persky value the present in opposition to the past, a conception of the dynamics of history that strikes me as more American than Jewish.

11. For the significance of geography to American self-understanding, see Myra Jehlen's *American Incarnation,* particularly the introduction and the first two chapters (1–122). Also see Mathy's *Extreme Occident* (163–206).

12. Paul Mendes-Flohr argues that the Jewish sense of history is not so much about the progression away from the past as an eternal recovery of the past. He quotes Franz Rosenzweig's observation that, for Israel, "the memory of its history does not form a point fixed in the past, a point which year after year becomes increasingly past. It is a memory which is really not past at all, but eternally present" (372).

13. See *Art and Ardor* (87–91), in which Ozick undertakes a powerful and disconcerting polemical rereading of Harold Bloom's understanding of literary history: powerful in its meticulous concern for detail and in its theologically informed understanding of traditional Jewish convictions about idolatry; disconcerting in that it is precisely a rereading of Bloom, a reading of Bloom against the grain. Ironically, Bloom stands as the powerful precursor who Ozick uses against himself. Displacing Bloom with Bloom's power. It is this kind of argumentative and fictive technique that has made Bloom consider Ozick as an exemplar of his own theorizing. As I have tried to show with the fiction, the similarities are striking, but Ozick is not placing herself over and against tradition, but using one tradition—or understanding of tradition—against another. History, memory, and tradition displace the timelessness of Bloom's romanticism.

Chapter 3. Re-membering the Body in the Work of Alice Walker

1. See especially the three essays collected in *Art and Ardor*: "The Hole/Birth Catalogue" (249–60), "Previsions of the Demise of the Dancing Dog" (263–83), and "Literature and the Politics of Sex: A Dissent" (284–90).

2. James Cone has pointed out that a constitutive feature of theological racism in America has been the conception of a white God, a conception accepted by many black churches (55–81). In the period to which the narrative speaks—the rural South following World War I—it is not surprising that Celie should need to free herself from these particular racist and sexist conceptions. Similar racist and sexist structures are present in Walker's own historical period. Dominant forms of Protestantism in many white churches have been ambiguous at best in their response to racism and have often been clearly hostile to the empowerment of women. Even religious circles that explicitly support efforts for black self-determination have advocated theological concepts or political strategies that have had implicit racist assumptions and consequences. King's "Letter from Birmingham Jail" provided an early analysis of this liberal ambiguity, and frustration over the inadequacy of liberal Christian responses to racism provoked James Cone to initiate the theological movement known as Black Theology (King 437–45, Cone 1–20).

3. For the best description of Celie as a slave, see Calvin Hernton.

4. On this point, Trudier Harris's complaints about Celie's voice and the horror that it obscures are well taken. That strength of voice must be transcended, or at least supplemented by actual change in Celie's situation (Harris, "Color Purple," 155–56). This places me somewhat at odds with those critics who see the voice in the letters as being the height of affirmation of Celie's individuality. The voice is a triumph, but Celie doesn't own it until she is economically independent. Thus voice itself, while something, doesn't count for much given the economic dependence that is Celie's life. In the same manner, her individuality,

while something, isn't the ultimate value sought in the novel. For a strong reading that emphasizes the strength and creativity of Celie's voice in the letters, see Henry Louis Gates (239–58), as well as Bonnie TuSmith (79–83). Often critics that emphasize the creativity of Celie's voice do so in contrast to Nettie's letters, written in a voice that they take to be contrived or somehow less "authentic." As I will make clear, I think this is a highly problematic reading, underplaying the significance of Nettie's letters to Celie's life, and implicitly dismissing the various voices with which black women, including Alice Walker, speak.

5. See especially the chapter "Notes on a Native Son" (97–111).

6. See Valerie Babb for a significant exception to the rule which seems to suggest that the novel begins to fall apart when Nettie's letters enter the picture.

7. For analysis of the ways in which African Americans have transformed a received Christianity, see Genovese 161–284, Cone 66–74.

8. See Judy Elsley for a study of the role of laughter in *The Color Purple*.

9. Throughout the novel Shug Avery uses the pronoun "It" to refer to God, an effort to get beyond referring to God as either exclusively male or female. The text uses uppercase and lowercase inconsistently with reference to this term. When quoting I have followed the text; in the context of my own discussion I have capitalized "It" and marked it with quotation marks.

10. In his *A Black Theology of Liberation,* James Cone points out that distinctions must be made between spiritual categories as they are applicable to the oppressed and as they are applicable to the oppressor. Thus, although Cone does not discuss celebration per se, his analysis would suggest that celebration is an expression of divine pleasure only when and if it is an expression of the oppressed. This would suggest that celebration by Albert, say, or by the white people of the town in *The Color Purple,* could only be a false joy—or at least a seriously compromised joy—because it is bought at the expense of Celie's misery and the misery of other black women in the novel. See Cone 21–39, 61–81.

Chapter 4. Memory, Place, and Ritual in Silko's Ceremony and Almanac of the Dead

1. See especially the video documentary *Leslie Marmon Silko,* directed by Matteo Bellinelli.

2. The tradition of the dialectic would place Pueblo traditionalism as the thesis that is transcended by modernity as the antithesis. Silko's work questions this chronological aspect of the dialectic, suggesting that Pueblo tradition does not belong simply to the past and that many aspects of that tradition serve as "antitheses" to modernity. Thus, as I suggested in my introduction, religion need not be thought of as simply a residual cultural formation, but rather one that is continually emergent.

3. Berger says: "[Because society is the guardian of order in its structuring of individual consciousness], radical separation from the social world, or anomy, constitutes . . . a powerful threat to the individual. It is not only that the individual loses emotionally satisfying ties in such cases. He loses his orientation in experience. In extreme cases, he loses his sense of reality and identity. He becomes anomic in the sense of becoming worldless. Just as an individual's nomos is constructed and sustained in conversation with significant others, so is the individual plunged toward anomy when such conversation is radically interrupted" (21–22).

4. This is quite close to Silko's personal memories of her own experiences in Indian schools. See Perry, 316–18.

5. I am drawing this notion of the effect of master narratives from Frank Lentricchia's discussion of anecdotes: "The teller of anecdotes has to presume the cultural currency of that large, containing biographical narrative which he draws upon for the sharp point he would give his anecdote, whose effect is ultimately political: to trigger a narrative sense of community that the anecdote evokes by evoking the master biography. In evoking the master biography, anecdote helps us to remember. And remembrance, so triggered, is the power which sustains, by retrieving, our basic cultural fiction" (321).

6. For the most significant works on the ideology of the land in the American and Native American imagination, see Stephen Cornell, *The Return of the Native;* Annette Kolodny, *The Lay of the Land;* Leo Marx, *The Machine in the Garden;* Henry Nash Smith, *Virgin Land.*

7. Silko has suggested persuasively that one reason the Pueblos have survived is that they have consistently appropriated resources from those who have tried to conquer them and have adapted those resources to their tribal traditions (Perry 316–17). Certainly it is the argument of this chapter that fictions are one such resource that Silko is adapting to Pueblo religious traditions.

8. Joseph Epes Brown describes the general character of these sandpainting ceremonies: "At a certain moment during the ceremony the ill person is placed at the center of one of the dry paintings; the understanding is that the person thus becomes identified with the power that is in the image painted on the earth with colored sand and pollen. And the singer takes some of the painted image and presses it to the body of the ill person, again to emphasize this element of identity: the painting is not a symbol of some meaning or power, the power *is* there present in it, and as the person identifies with it the appropriate cure is accomplished" ("Becoming" 20).

9. Silko disparages the Manichaean political rhetoric of some Indian political groups. Of AIM, she says, "Radical Indian politicians like to say, 'Well, it's all the white people's fault, you know, we didn't do any of this.' That's such a simplistic view, because from the very beginning, the betrayals of our people occurred through deeply complicated convergences of intentions and world

views. And there were persons, full-blood Indians, who cooperated with the enemy or who cooperated with the invaders, and there were mixed blood or 'half-breed' people who did—that's human nature. . . . It is not just one group of people, that's too simple" (Seyersted, "Two Interviews," 32).

10. Silko suggests that, in a sense, she believes the land itself is telling the story. This would be consonant with her belief that the story is being given her by Pueblo gods who themselves cannot be separated from the earth (*Delicacy* 27).

11. For discussion of the role of Ts'eh in *Ceremony*, see Allen, *The Sacred Hoop*, 118; Judith Antell, 219; Edith Swan, "Symbolic Geography," 242–46. Swan does the best job of going beyond simplistically psychologizing Ts'eh's role in Tayo's life. For other essays that detail the significance of Yellow Woman to Silko generally, and specifically to her short story of the same name, see Graulich. For an anthropological description of the role of Yellow Woman, see Tyler 78, 166, 188–89.

12. Silko has emphasized storytelling as being the basis for personal and communal creation. "[T]hat's how you know you belong, if the stories incorporate you into them. There have to be stories. It's stories that make this a community. People tell those stories about you and your family or about others and they begin to create your identity. In a sense, you are told who you are, or you know who you are by the stories that are told about you" (Evers and Carr 29–30, quoted in Graulich 5).

13. See Matteo Bellinelli's documentary *Leslie Marmon Silko*.

Chapter 5. Chanting the Descent Lines: Maxine Hong Kingston's The Woman Warrior

1. Stephen Teiser articulates the difficulty of vocabulary in speaking about Chinese religions. On the one hand, concepts like popular religion have a Western ring to them designed to distinguish the practice of the masses from the official ritual and theologies of institutional churches. Similarly, the language for Chinese relationships to ancestors is notoriously difficult. In the missionary period these practices were described as "ancestor worship." More recent anthropologists have designated such practices as "the cult of the dead" to indicate that the ancestors are not thought of as gods, as might be assumed by a word like *worship*. I am equally uncomfortable with the phrase *cult of the dead* simply because I believe that, in America at least, it calls up as many if not more negative connotations than its predecessor, *ancestor worship*. To negotiate these difficulties, I have decided to use the term *ancestor reverence* to describe practices designed to maintain relationships between the living and the dead, and I will make occasional use of the term *popular religion*, though I will mostly refer simply to either Confucianism or Chinese religion. I believe that those aspects of Chinese popular religion and Confucianism that I am emphasizing—obligation

to others that is so extensive it becomes a de facto metaphysical ground—are so closely related that the distinctions between popular and official religion are largely unimportant for this study.

2. Kingston makes this case in "Cultural Mis-readings by American Reviewers." Oddly, the same charge is made by Frank Chan in his repudiation of a reviewer of *Woman Warrior* and by Benjamin Tong in his review of the book. Both Chan and Tong believe that Kingston invites misreadings of Chinese culture by emphasizing its exotic character. (See Sau-ling Cynthia Wong, "Necessity and Extravagance," 3–4, for a discussion of these charges against Kingston.)

3. See my discussion in chapter 4 on Leslie Marmon Silko, as well as my more general discussion of Berger in chapter 1.

4. My discussion at this point shouldn't be taken to mean that such patriarchal structures are unique to China. As Simone de Beauvoir points out, these kinds of structures are to some degree common to patriarchy everywhere. Indeed, visiting the Promise Keepers rally in Washington, D.C., in the fall of 1997, I was impressed by the iterated formula that "strong families make strong neighborhood make strong communities make strong states make a strong nation." Perhaps what makes the American context distinct here is not so much the structure of patriarchal belief as the peculiar turns and developments this formula took in China. Among other things, the American distinction between private and public life has tended to curb, though not eliminate, the continuities that were in place between religion, state, and family life in traditional China.

5. The literature on silencing in Kingston's work is overwhelming, and I am especially indebted to King-Kok Cheung and Linda Morante in this regard. My concern in this chapter is not to dispute the things in Kingston that despair at the silencing strategies in Chinese and Chinese American cultures, but rather to suggest that gender and ethnicity cannot be readily opposed as they seem to be by both Cheung and Morante, as well as by Linda Hunt. Such a dichotomy supports, too readily I think, the thesis that Kingston falls into some kind of ethnic or racial self-hatred, the theses promoted by Frank Chan, Frank Chin ("Autobiography"), and Benjamin Tong. (See Wong for a discussion of Chan and Tong.)

6. The exclusion laws against Chinese immigrants most often focused on keeping Chinese women from joining the men who had immigrated to the United States as workers in the nineteenth and early twentieth century. Thus the Chinese American culture that first developed in the United States was almost exclusively male. Kingston's *China Men* is, in part, an excellent imaginative reconstruction of this period of Chinese American culture.

WORKS CITED

Allen, Paula Gunn. "The Psychological Landscape of *Ceremony.*" *American Indian Quarterly* 5 (Feb. 1979): 7–12.

———. *The Sacred Hoop.* Boston: Beacon, 1986.

Anderson, Benedict. *Imagined Communities: Reflections on the Origin and Spread of Nationalism.* Rev. ed. New York: Verso Press, 1983, 1991.

Antell, Judith. "Momaday, Welch, Silko: Expressing the Feminine Principle Through Male Alienation." *American Indian Quarterly* 7 (Summer, 1988): 213–20.

Asad, Talal. *Genealogies of Religion: Discipline and Reasons of Power in Christianity and Islam.* Baltimore: Johns Hopkins Univ. Press, 1993.

Babb, Valerie. "Women and Words: Articulating the Self in *Their Eyes Were Watching God* and *The Color Purple.*" *Alice Walker and Zora Neale Hurston: The Common Bond.* Ed. Lillie P. Howard. Westport, Conn.: Greenwood Press, 1993. 83–93.

Baer, Hans A., and Merrill Singer. *African-American Religion in the Twentieth Century: Varieties of Protest and Accommodation.* Knoxville: Univ. of Tennessee Press, 1992.

Barnes, Kim. "A Leslie Marmon Silko Interview." *"Yellow Woman": Leslie Marmon Silko.* Ed. Melody Graulich. New Brunswick, N.J.: Rutgers Univ. Press, 1993. 47–65.

Bellah, Robert. *Beyond Belief.* New York: Harper and Row, 1976.

Bellah, Robert, et al. *Habits of the Heart: Individualism and Commitment in American Life.* Berkeley: Univ. of California Press, 1985.

Benjamin, Walter. *Illuminations.* Trans. Harry Zohn. Ed. Hannah Arendt. New York: Schocken, 1968.

Berger, Peter L. *The Sacred Canopy: Elements of a Sociological Theory of Religion.* New York: Doubleday, 1967.

Bhabha, Homi. *The Location of Culture.* London: Routledge, 1994.

Bloom, Harold. *The American Religion: The Emergence of the Post-Christian Nation.* New York: Simon and Schuster, 1992.

———. *The Anxiety of Influence: A Theory of Poetry.* New York: Oxford Univ. Press, 1973.

———, ed. *Cynthia Ozick.* New York: Chelsea House, 1986.

Bowers, Neal, and Charles L. P. Silet. "An Interview with Gerald Vizenor." *MELUS* 8 (Spring 1981): 41–49.

Branch, Taylor. *Parting the Waters: America in the King Years, 1954–1963.* New York: Simon and Schuster, 1988.

Brown, Joseph Epes. "Becoming Part of It." *I Become Part of It: Sacred Dimension in Native American Life.* Ed. D. M. Dooling and Paul Jordan-Smith. New York: Parabola Books, 1989. 9–20.

———. *The Spiritual Legacy of the American Indian.* New York: Crossroad, 1982.

Candelaria, Cordelia Chavez. "Difference and the Discourse of 'Community' in Writings by and about the Ethnic Other(s)." *An Other Tongue: Nation and Ethnicity in the Linguistic Borderlands.* Ed. Alfred Arteaga. Duke Univ. Press, Durham, 1994. 185–202.

Castillo, Ana. *Massacre of the Dreamers: Essays on Xicanisma.* New York: Penguin, 1995.

Cheung, King-Kok. "'Don't Tell': Imposed Silences in *The Color Purple* and *The Woman Warrior.*" *PMLA* 103 (Mar. 1988): 162–74.

Chin, Frank. "This Is Not an Autobiography." *Genre* 18.2 (1985): 109–30.

Christ, Carol. *Diving Deep and Surfacing: Women Writers on a Spiritual Quest.* 2d ed. Boston: Beacon, 1986 (1980).

Cleaver, Eldridge. *Soul on Ice.* New York: Dell, 1968.

Cohen, Arthur. *The Natural and Supernatural Jew.* 2d ed. New York: Berhman House, 1962, 1979.

Cohen, Arthur A., and Paul Mendes-Flohr, eds. *Contemporary Jewish Religious Thought: Original Essays on Critical Concepts, Movements, and Beliefs.* New York: Scribner's, 1987.

Cohen, Sarah. *Cynthia Ozick's Comic Art: From Levity to Liturgy.* Bloomington: Indiana Univ. Press, 1994.

Cone, James H. *A Black Theology of Liberation.* 20th anniv. ed. Maryknoll, New York: Orbis, 1990.

Cornell, Stephen. *The Return of the Native: American Indian Political Resurgence*. New York: Oxford Univ. Press, 1988.

Culler, Jonathan. *Framing the Sign: Criticism and Its Institutions*. Norman: Univ. of Oklahoma Press, 1988.

De Beauvoir, Simone. "Introduction to *The Second Sex*." *New French Feminisms*. New York: Schocken, 1981. 41–56.

Deloria, Vine. "Out of Chaos." *I Become Part of It: Sacred Dimension in Native American Life*. Eds. D. M. Dooling and Paul Jordan-Smith. New York: Parabola, 1989: 259–69.

———. *God Is Red*. New York: Grossett Dunlap, 1973.

Detweiler, Robert. *Breaking the Fall: Religious Readings of Contemporary Fiction*. San Francisco: Harper & Row, 1989.

Douglas, Ann. *The Feminization of American Culture*. New York: Knopf, 1977.

Douglass, Frederick. *Narrative of the Life of Frederick Douglass: An American Slave*. New York: Penguin, 1982.

Du Bois, W. E. B. *The Souls of Black Folk*. *Writings*. Ed. Nathan Huggins. New York: Literary Classics of the United States, Library of America. 357–47.

Eliade, Mircea. *The Sacred and the Profane: The Nature of Religion*. Trans. Willard R. Trask. New York: Harcourt, 1959.

Elliot, Emory et al., ed. *Columbia Literary History of the United States*. New York: Columbia Univ. Press, 1988.

Elsley, Judy. "Laughter as Feminine Power in *The Color Purple* and *A Question of Silence*." *New Perspectives on Woman and Comedy*. Ed. Regina Barreca. Philadelphia: Gordon and Breach, 1992. 193–99.

Evers, Larry, and Denny Carr. "A Conversation with Leslie Marmon Silko." *Sun Tracks* 3:1 (Fall 1976): 29–30.

Finkelstein, Norman. *The Ritual of New Creation: Jewish Tradition and Contemporary Literature*. Albany: State Univ. of New York Press, 1992.

Fishbane, Michael, ed. *The Midrashic Imagination: Jewish Exegesis, Thought, and History*. Albany: State Univ. of New York Press, 1993.

Frazier, E. Franklin. *The Negro Church in America*. New York: Schocken Books, 1974.

Garrett, Jimmy. "We Own the Night." *Black Fire: An Anthology of Afro-American Writing*. Ed. Leroi Jones (Amiri Baraka) and Larry Neal. New York: William Morrow, 1968. 527–40.

Gates, Henry Louis, Jr. *The Signifying Monkey: A Theory of Afro-American Literary Criticism*. New York: Oxford Univ. Press, 1988.

Gates, Henry Louis, Jr., Nellie McKay et al., eds. *The Norton Anthology of African American Literature*. New York: W. W. Norton, 1997.

Gates, Hill. "The Commoditization of Chinese Women." *Signs* 14 (1989): 799–832.

Genovese, Eugene D. *Roll, Jordan, Roll: The World the Slaves Made*. New York: Random House, 1974.

Giddings, Paula. *When and Where I Enter: The Impact of Black Women on Race and Sex in America*. New York: William Morrow, 1984.

Glazer, Nathan. *American Judaism*. Chicago: Univ. of Chicago Press, 1957.

Grant, Jacquelyn. "Black Women and the Church." *All the Women Are White, All the Blacks Are Men, but Some of Us Are Brave: Black Women's Studies*. Ed. Gloria T. Hull, Patricia Bell Scott, and Barbara Smith. Old Westbury, N.Y.: Feminist, 1982. 141–46.

Graulich, Melody ed. *"Yellow Woman": Leslie Marmon Silko*. New Brunswick, N.J.: Rutgers Univ. Press, 1993.

Gunn, Giles. *The Interpretation of Otherness: Literature, Religion, and the American Imagination*. New York: Oxford Univ. Press, 1979.

Gutjahr, Paul C. *An American Bible: A History of the Good Book in the United States, 1777–1880*. Stanford: Stanford Univ. Press, 1999.

Harap, Louis. *In the Mainstream: The Jewish Presence in Twentieth-Century American Literature, 1950s–1980s*. New York: Greenwood, n.d.

Harris, Trudier. "From Exile to Asylum: Religion and Community in the Writings of Contemporary Black Women." *Women's Writing in Exile*. Eds. Mary Lynn Broe and Angela Ingram. Chapel Hill: Univ. of North Carolina Press, 1989. 151–69.

———. "From Victimization to Free Enterprise: Alice Walker's *The Color Purple*." *Studies in American Fiction* 14 (Spring 1986): 1–18.

———. "On *The Color Purple*, Stereotypes, and Silence." *Black American Literary Forum* 18 (Winter 1984): 155–61.

Hart, Ray L. *Unfinished Man and the Imagination*. New York: Herder, 1968. New York: Seabury, 1979.

Heinemann, Joseph. "The Nature of Aggadah." *Midrash and Literature*. Eds. Geoffrey H. Hartman and Sanford Budick. New Haven: Yale Univ. Press, 1986. 41–55.

Hernton, Calvin. *The Sexual Mountain and Black Women Writers.* New York: Anchor-Doubleday, 1987.

Hertzberg, Arthur. *The Jews in America: Four Centuries of an Uneasy Encounter: A History.* New York: Simon and Schuster, 1989.

Hill, Patricia Liggins et al., eds. *Call and Response: The Riverside Anthology of the African American Literary Tradition.* Boston: Houghton Mifflin, 1998.

Hobson, Geary, ed. *The Remembered Earth: An Anthology of Contemporary Native American Literature.* Albuquerque: Red Earth, 1979.

hooks, bell. *Yearning: Race, Gender, and Cultural Politics.* Boston: South End, 1990.

Huggins, Nathan Irvin, ed. *Voices from the Harlem Renaissance.* New York: Oxford Univ. Press, 1976.

Hughes, Langston. "Goodbye Christ." *Voices from the Harlem Renaissance.* Ed. Nathan Irvin Huggins. New York: Oxford Univ. Press, 1976. 419–20.

Hunt, Linda. "I Could Not Figure Out What Was My Village": Gender Vs. Ethnicity in Maxine Hong Kingston's *The Woman Warrior.*" *MELUS* 12 (Fall 1985): 5–12.

Jameson, Fredric. *The Political Unconscious: Narrative as a Socially Symbolic Act.* Ithaca, N.Y.: Cornell Univ. Press, 1981.

————. *Postmodernism: Or, the Cultural Logic of Late Capitalism.* Durham, N.C.: Duke Univ. Press, 1991.

————. "The Realist Floorplan." *On Signs.* Ed. Marshall Blonsky. Baltimore: Johns Hopkins Univ. Press, 1985. 373–83.

Jehlen, Myra. *American Incarnation: The Individual, the Nation, and the Continent.* Cambridge, Mass.: Harvard Univ. Press, 1986.

Jones, Leroi (Baraka, Amiri), and Larry Neal eds. *Black Fire: An Anthology of Afro-American Writing.* New York: William Morrow, 1968.

Kauvar, Elaine. *Cynthia Ozick's Fiction: Tradition and Invention.* Bloomington: Indiana Univ. Press, 1993.

Kessner, Carole, ed. *The "Other" New York Jewish Intellectuals.* New York: New York Univ. Press, 1994.

Kim, Elaine H. *Asian American Literature: An Introduction to the Writings and Their Social Context.* Philadelphia: Temple Univ. Press, 1982.

King, Martin Luther, Jr. "Letter from Birmingham Jail—April 16, 1963." *Afro-American Religious History: A Documentary Witness.* Ed. Milton C. Sernett. Durham, N.C.: Duke Univ. Press, 1985. 430–45.

Kingston, Maxine Hong. *China Men.* New York: Random House, 1989.

———. "Cultural Mis-readings by American Reviewers." *Asian and Western Writers in Dialogue.* Ed. Guy Amirthanayagam. London: Macmillan, 1982. 55–65.

———. "Reservations About China." *Ms.* 7 (Oct. 1978): 67–68.

———. *Tripmaster Monkey: His Fakebook.* New York: Random House, 1990.

———. *The Woman Warrior: Memoirs of a Girlhood Among Ghosts.* New York: Random House, 1989, 1976.

Kolodny, Annette. *The Lay of the Land: Metaphor as Experience and History in American Life and Letters.* Chapel Hill: Univ. of North Carolina Press, 1975.

Lauter, Paul, gen. ed. *The Heath Anthology of American Literature.* Lexington, Mass.: D. C. Heath, 1990.

Lentricchia, Frank. "In Place of an Afterword—Someone Reading." *Critical Terms for Literary Study.* Ed. Frank Lentricchia and Thomas McLaughlin. Chicago: Univ. of Chicago Press, 1990. 321–38.

Leslie Marmon Silko. Film. Dir. Matteo Bellinelli. Written by Andrea Belloni, Claudo Belotti, et al. Princeton: Films for the Humanities & Sciences, 1995.

Lincoln, C. Eric. *The Black Church Since Frazier.* New York: Schocken, 1974.

Ling, Amy. *Between Worlds: Women Writers of Chinese Ancestry.* New York: Pergamon, 1990.

Lipsitz, George. *Time Passages: Collective Memory and American Popular Culture.* Minneapolis: Univ. of Minneapolis Press, 1990.

Lopez, Donald S. Jr., ed. *Asian Religions in Practice.* Princeton: Princeton Univ. Press, 1999.

Lorde, Audre. "The Master's Tools Will Never Dismantle the Master's House." *Sister Outsider.* Trumansburge, N.Y.: Crossing, 1984. 110–13.

Lowin, Joseph. *Cynthia Ozick.* Boston: Twayne, 1988.

MacIntyre, Alasdair. *Whose Justice? Which Rationality?* South Bend, Ind.: Univ. Notre Dame Press, 1988.

Marty, Martin ed. *Ethnic and Non-Protestant Themes.* New York: K. G. Saur, 1993.

———. "Skeleton of Religion." *The Immigrant Religious Experience.* Ed. George E. Pozzetta. New York: Garland, 1991. 225–41.

Marx, Leo. *The Machine in the Garden: Technology and the Pastoral Ideal in America.* New York: Oxford Univ. Press, 1964.

Mathy, Jean-Philippe. *Extrême-Occident: French Intellectuals and America.* Chicago: Univ. of Chicago Press, 1993.

May, Henry F. "Religion and American Intellectual History, 1945–1985: Reflections on an Uneasy Relationship." *Religion and Twentieth-Century American Intellectual Life.* Ed. Michael J. Lacy. Cambridge: Cambridge Univ. Press, 1989. 12–22.

McGrane, Bernard. *Beyond Anthropology: Society and the Other.* New York: Columbia Univ. Press, 1989.

McQuade, Donald, et al., eds. *The Harper American Literature.* Compact ed. New York: Harper and Row, 1987.

Mendes-Flohr, Paul. "History." *Contemporary Jewish Religious Thought: Original Essays on Critical Concepts, Movements, and Beliefs.* Eds. Arthur A. Cohen and Paul Mendes-Flohr. New York: Scribner's, 1987. 371–87.

Molesworth, Charles. "Culture, Power, and Society." *Columbia Literary History of the United States.* Ed. Emory Elliot, et al. New York: Columbia Univ. Press, 1988. 1023–44.

Morante, Linda. "From Silence to Song: The Triumph of Maxine Hong Kingston." *Frontiers* 9.2 (1987): 78–82.

Morrison, Toni. *Beloved.* New York: Knopf, 1987.

Neusner, Jacob. *A Midrash Reader.* Minneapolis: Fortress, 1990.

Orr, Robert G. *Religion in China.* New York: Friendship, 1980.

Overmeyer, Daniel L. *Religions of China: The World as Living System.* New York: Harper Row, 1986.

Ozick, Cynthia. *Art and Ardor.* New York: Knopf, 1983.

———. *Bloodshed and Three Novellas.* New York: Dutton, 1983.

———. *Levitation: Five Fictions.* New York: Dutton, 1983.

———. *The Messiah of Stockholm.* New York: Random House, 1988.

———. *Metaphor and Memory.* New York: Knopf, 1989.

———. *The Pagan Rabbi and Other Stories.* New York: Schocken, 1976.

———. *The Shawl.* New York: Random House, 1990.

Perry, Donna. *Backtalk: Women Writers Speak Out.* New Brunswick, N.J.: Rutgers Univ. Press, 1993.

Phillips, Derek L. *Looking Backward : A Critical Appraisal of Communitarian Thought.* Princeton: Princeton Univ. Press, 1993.

Pifer, Ellen. "Cynthia Ozick; Invention and Orthodoxy." *Contemporary American Women Writers: Narrative Strategies*. Ed. Catherine Rainwater and William J. Scheick. Lexington: Univ. Press of Kentucky, 1985. 89–109.

Pryse, Marjorie. "Zora Neale Hurston, Alice Walker, and the 'Ancient Power' of Black Women." *Conjuring: Black Women, Fiction, and Literary Tradition*. Ed. Marjorie Pryse and Hortense J. Spillers. Bloomington: Indiana Univ. Press, 1985. 1–24.

Rabinowitz, Paula. "Eccentric Memories: A Conversation with Maxine Hong Kingston." *Michigan Quarterly Review* 26 (Winter 1987): 177–87.

Raschke, Carl. "Theorizing Religion at the Turn of the Millennium: From the Sacred to the Semiotic." *Journal for Cultural and Religious Theory* 1.1 (Dec. 1999). http://www.jcrt.org/archives/01.1/index.html?page=raschke.html.

Rich, Adrienne. *Adrienne Rich's Poetry*. Ed. Barbara Charlesworth Gelpi and Albert Gelpi. New York: W. W. Norton, 1975.

Rodriguez, Richard. *Hunger of Memory: The Education of Richard Rodriguez: An Autobiography*. New York: Bantam Books, 1983.

Roth, Philip. *Goodbye Columbus*. New York: Random House, 1959, 1987.

Rubenstein, Richard L. *After Auschwitz: History, Theology, and Contemporary Judaism*. 2d ed. Baltimore: Johns Hopkins Univ. Press, 1966, 1992.

Ruether, Rosemary Radford. *Sexism and God-Talk: Toward a Feminist Theology*. Boston: Beacon, 1983.

Scholem, Gershom. *Kabbalah*. New York: New American Library, 1974.

———. *The Messianic Idea in Judaism and Other Essays on Jewish Spirituality*. New York: Schocken, 1971.

Seyersted, Per. "Two Interviews with Leslie Marmon Silko." *American Studies in Scandinavia* 13 (1981): 17–33.

Silko, Leslie Marmon. *Almanac of the Dead*. New York: Simon and Schuster, 1991.

———. "An Old Time Indian Attack: Conducted in Two Parts." *The Remembered Earth: An Anthology of Contemporary Native American Literature*. Ed. Geary Hobson, 211–16. Albuquerque: Red Earth, 1979.

———. *Ceremony*. New York: Signet, 1977.

———. "Landscape, History, and the Pueblo Imagination." *On Nature*. Ed. David Halpern, 83–94. San Francisco: North Point, 1987.

———. *Yellow Woman and a Beauty of the Spirit: Essays on Native American Life Today*. New York: Simon and Schuster, 1996.

Silko, Leslie Marmon, and James Wright. *The Delicacy and Strength of Lace: Letters between Leslie Marmon Silko and James Wright.* Ed. Anne Wright. Saint Paul, Minn.: Graywolf, 1986.

Smith, Henry Nash. *Virgin Land: The American West as Symbol and Myth.* Cambridge: Harvard Univ. Press, 1950.

Stange, Mary Zeiss. "Treading the Narrative Way between Myth and Madness: Maxine Hong Kingston and Contemporary Women's Autobiography." *Journal of Feminist Studies in Religion* 3 (Spring, 1987): 15–28.

Stephanson, Anders. "Regarding Postmodernism—A Conversation with Frederic Jameson." *Universal Abandon? The Politics of Postmodernism.* Ed. Andrew Ross. Minneapolis: Univ. of Minnesota Press, 1988. 3–30.

Stowe, Harriet Beecher. *Three Novels.* New York: Literary Classics of the United States, Library of America, 1982.

Strandberg, Victor. *Greek Mind and Jewish Soul: The Conflicted Art of Cynthia Ozick.* Madison: Univ. of Wisconsin Press, 1994.

Swan, Edith. "Laguna Symbolic Geography and Silko's Ceremony." *American Indian Quarterly* 12 (Summer 1988): 229–49.

Teiser, Stephen F. "Religions of China in Practice." *Asian Religions in Practice.* Ed. Donald S. Lopez, Jr. Princeton: Princeton Univ. Press, 1999. 88–122.

Thompson, Robert Farris. *Flash of the Spirit: African and Afro-American Art and Philosophy.* New York: Random House, 1984.

Toelken, Barre. "The Demands of Harmony." *I Become Part of It: Sacred Dimension in Native American Life.* Ed. D. M. Dooling and Paul Jordan-Smith. New York: Parabola Books, 1989. 59–74.

Tompkins, Jane. *Sensational Designs: The Cultural Work of American Fiction, 1790–1850.* New York: Oxford Univ. Press, 1985.

Tsai, Shih-Shan Henry. *The Chinese Experience in America.* Bloomington: Indiana Univ. Press, 1986.

TuSmith, Bonnie. *All My Relatives: Community in Contemporary Ethnic American Literatures.* Ann Arbor: Univ. of Michigan Press, 1993.

Tyler, Hamilton A. *Pueblo Gods and Myths.* Norman: Univ. of Oklahoma Press, 1964.

Updike, John. *Bech: A Book.* New York: Knopf, 1970.

———. *Picked Up Pieces.* New York: Knopf, 1975.

Velie, Alan R. ed. *American Indian Literature: An Anthology.* Norman: Univ. of Oklahoma Press, 1979.

Walker, Alice. *By the Light of My Father's Smile*. New York: Random House, 1998.

——. *The Color Purple*. New York: Simon and Schuster, 1982.

——. *In Search of Our Mothers' Gardens*. New York: Harcourt, 1984.

——. *Living By the Word*. New York: Harcourt, 1989.

——. *Meridian*. New York: Simon and Schuster, 1976.

——. *Possessing the Secret of Joy*. New York: Harcourt, 1992.

——. *Revolutionary Petunias and Other Poems*. New York: Harcourt, 1973.

——. *The Temple of My Familiar*. New York: Simon and Schuster, 1989.

Wallace, Michele. *Black Macho and the Myth of the Superwoman*. New York: Dial, 1979.

Wiesel, Elie. *The Kingdom of Memory*. New York: Summit Books, 1990.

Williams, Raymond. *Marxism and Literature*. New York: Oxford Univ. Press, 1977.

Wilmore, Gayraud S. *Black Religions and Black Radicalism*. 2d ed. Maryknoll, New York: Orbis, 1983.

Winsbro, Bonnie. *Supernatural Forces: Belief, Difference, and Power in Contemporary Works by Ethnic Women*. Amherst: Univ. of Massachusetts Press, 1993.

Wong, Sau-ling Cynthia. "Autobiography as Guided Chinatown Tour?: Maxine Hong Kingston's *The Woman Warrior* and the Chinese-American Autobiographical Controversy." *Multicultural Autobiography: American Lives*. Ed. James Robert Payne. Knoxville: Univ. of Tennessee Press, 1992. 248–79.

——. "Necessity and Extravagance in Maxine Hong Kingston's *The Woman Warrior*." *MELUS* 15 (Spring 1988): 3–26.

X, Malcolm, and Alex Haley. *The Autobiography of Malcolm X*. New York: Grove, 1966.

Yang, C. K. *Religion in Chinese Society*. Berkeley: Univ. of California Press, 1961.

Yerushalmi, Yosef Hayim. *Zakhor: Jewish History and Jewish Memory*. Philadelphia: The Jewish Publication Society of America in cooperation with Seattle and London: Univ. of Washington Press, 1982.

Yezierska, Anzia. *Bread Givers: A Struggle between a Father of the Old World and a Daughter of the New*. New York: Persea, 1970, 1925.

INDEX

Recalling Religions was designed and typeset on a Macintosh computer system using Quark software. The text is set in Sabon and the chapter openings are set in Optima. This book was designed and typeset by Bill Adams and manufactured by Thomson-Shore, Inc. The paper used in this book is designed for an effective life of at least three hundred years.